SECRETS OF
FLY-FISHING
FOR TROUT

For my parents
William and Joan,
with love and affection.

SECRETS OF FLY-FISHING FOR TROUT

Ian Ball

RIGHT WAY

CONTENTS

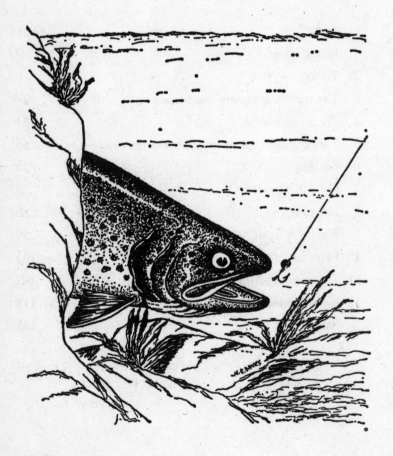

1. Brown trout

1

INTRODUCTION

Welcome to the magnificent and exhilarating sport of fly-fishing for trout!

This great little fact-packed book explores the wonderful and exciting underwater world of the trout; teaches how best to locate and catch large trout using the right tackle, artificial flies and fly-fishing techniques, and gives priceless information, hints and tips to help *you* catch more and even bigger trout in the months and years ahead!

This book provides an excellent introduction to the sporting pursuit of trout living in the flowing waters of rivers and streams; the still-waters of small natural lakes; man-made fisheries; ponds, pits, lakes; and the still-waters of reservoirs, large natural lakes, Scottish lochs and Irish loughs.

Also included are extremely helpful and informative reference sections, which should prove valuable and beneficial throughout your fly-fishing lifetime.

Where to fly-fish?
Begin with a visit to your local fishing tackle dealer.

Tackle dealers
For accurate, knowledgeable, up-to-date information

about the availability of inexpensive fly-fishing in your locality, visit the local fishing tackle dealer, who will be delighted to furnish details of the licence/permit/ticket required to fly-fish for trout on local waters, give tips on the best artificial flies to use for bonus catches of big trout, and supply any items of fly-fishing tackle you may require.

Magazines and newspapers

Read fly-fishing magazines and the fly-fishing sections of angling newspapers for information about the latest exciting developments on different trout waters; details of new tackle, techniques and innovative patterns of artificial trout-flies to buy or tie, and try for yourself.

Angling clubs

To make the finest possible start in the thrilling sport of fly-fishing for trout, join an angling club which offers expert instruction in fly-fishing, and organizes regular fly-fishing trips to top trout waters.

To succeed

To achieve consistent fly-fishing success, *specialize* in fly-fishing on one or two trout waters each year; learn the best spots to locate trout and the most successful techniques and artificial flies to use.

Aim to learn something new each outing.

Keep detailed notes in a fly-fishing diary or logbook, which fast becomes a personal gold mine of trout-hooking hints, tips and wisdom to help increase your catch rate of specimen trout.

ABOVE ALL: BE PATIENT AND PERSISTENT TO SUCCEED.

2

TROUT

Trout are prized by anglers for their superb sporting qualities, and valued by many peoples of the world for their culinary and nutritional excellence.

The trout has been transported and stocked in suitable waters around the world. Today trout are found in every continent except Antarctica.

Trout belong to the salmon *(Salmonidae)* family of freshwater fish. The trout is native to Europe, Asia and North America.

Although trout vary widely in size and colour there are only three distinctly different species of trout:

(a) Brown trout *(Salmo trutta)* of Europe and Asia.

(b) Rainbow trout *(Salmo gairdneri)* of North America.

(c) Cutthroat trout *(Salmo clarki)* of North America.

The cutthroat trout *(Salmo clarki)*, native to North America, and named after the bright red markings across its throat; giving the superficial appearance of a cut throat, is not found in British waters.

Trout found in British waters
The native British trout is the brown trout *(Salmo trutta)*. Brown trout vary considerably in size and colour according to the water in which they live; camouflage colours

2. Brown trout

blend with underwater surroundings and range from the yellow-brown-silver bodied, brightly speckled brown trout of bright-gravelbed waters, to the almost black colour of brown trout living in peaty-dark moorland waters.

Brown trout living in the still-waters of large lakes, Scottish lochs and Irish loughs vary in size and colour from one water to another, and sometimes the colour of brown trout varies within the same water, influenced by the predominant colours of the underwater areas over which the trout normally feed, and type of food preferred: trout feeding primarily on crustaceans such as *daphnia* (water-fleas), or freshwater shrimps, develop especially bright red and orange markings.

3. Scottish loch trout

The size of a fully-grown mature trout is affected by:
(a) The availability of nutritious natural food.
(b) The amount of energy the trout has to expend to catch the food.
(c) The size and depth of water.

Brown trout *(Salmo trutta)*
Brown trout living in fast flowing small streams use considerable energy holding position and swimming against the current. Mature small-stream brown trout may

rarely exceed 227g (½ lb) in weight.

Brown trout living in clean, well-oxygenated rivers which maintain a reasonably constant water level and plentiful supply of food, can exceed 2.27kg (5 lb) in weight.

Brown trout living in rivers and streams are solitary, territorial fish, prepared to defend their chosen territory, called a *lie*.

Brown trout choose a lie offering security from predators, shelter from the current, and easy access to natural food carried on the current.

Favourite lies include: bank undercuts, holes or hollows; beneath overhanging trees, shrubs and submerged tree roots; behind submerged rocks, boulders/large stones, clumps of weed; in deep pools of water.

Brown trout living in the still-waters of lakes, reservoirs, pits and ponds are less solitary and territorial than those brown trout living in rivers and streams.

There is little or no current in still-waters to bring trout a steady supply of natural food, so brown trout living in still-waters cannot rely on food-productive lies.

Brown trout living in still-waters must travel widely in search of prey and might cover considerable distances in the course of a day; though some find and frequent their own favourite feeding spots.

Brown trout living in *food-rich* large still-waters (lakes, reservoirs, Scottish lochs and Irish loughs) can exceed 4.5kg (10 lb) in weight.

Sea trout *(Salmo trutta)*
Sea trout are brown trout that have chosen to live in the sea; returning to rivers and streams to breed *(spawn)*.

Sea trout develop a bright silver colour, speckled with dark spots.

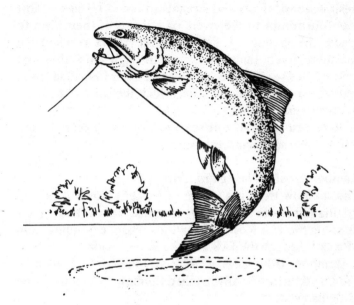

4. Sea trout

At sea the sea trout feed in shoals and enjoy a high protein diet including: sprats, sand eels, young herrings, small fish, crabs, shrimps and prawns.

Rich sea-feeding results in rapid weight gain, and sea trout can double their original freshwater weight after one year at sea. The longer they live at sea the larger sea trout grow.

Sea trout can exceed 13.61kg (30 lb) in weight, though the majority caught with rod and line in rivers and streams scale between 1.36kg (3 lb) and 4.53kg (10 lb) in weight.

After about 2–4 years at sea, the sea trout return to the fresh water of rivers and streams to breed *(spawn)*. Most sea trout return to the rivers or streams of their birth to spawn, navigating by taste once they have reached the coastal region of the river estuary through which they first entered the sea. The fresh water of each individual river and stream has a unique *taste*, which the sea trout is able to discern and follow.

Some sea trout stay at sea for 5 or more years before returning to spawn in fresh water.

Rainbow trout *(Salmo gairdneri)*
The rainbow trout is a native of western North America, originating from the swift streams, lakes and rivers draining the vast Rocky Mountains range, extending from Mexico, through the U.S.A., and into Canada.

Rainbow trout eggs were first shipped to Britain in 1884, and the artificially hatched rainbow trout introduced to British waters.

Rainbow trout grow at twice the speed of brown trout, and after two years can top 2.72kg (6 lb) in weight.

Rainbow trout living in the large still-waters of lakes and reservoirs can exceed 6.80kg (15 lb) in weight.

The rainbow trout rarely breeds naturally in Britain and normally lives only 4–7 years.

The mature rainbow trout is a feast of colour: blue-green, silvery back with black spots; a shimmering rainbow-like flash of purple along its silvery-white, black-speckled body.

In Britain, the rainbow trout is bred under artificial conditions by fish farms for stocking in rivers, streams, lakes, reservoirs, pits and ponds.

Rainbow trout thrive in the same waters as brown trout.

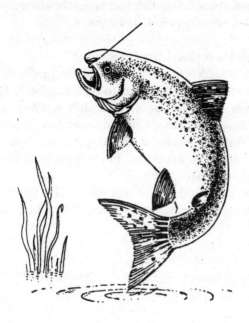

5. Rainbow trout

The rainbow trout, a non-territorial fish, roves widely in search of food.

Unlike brown trout, the rainbow trout in rivers and streams seldom seek favourite lies from which to seize food carried to them on the current. Rainbow trout hunt a wide variety of food across considerable distances, feeding voraciously from water bottom to water surface throughout the day.

A mature rainbow trout can conscientiously feed its way along 0.80km (½ mile) of water within 60 minutes.

Rainbow trout are sociable fish and often shoal together in search of food, especially in still-waters.

American brook trout *(Salvelinus fontinalis)*
The American brook trout *(Salvelinus fontinalis)* was misnamed by early British migrants to New England. The American brook trout is not a trout, but a **Char** and belongs to the *Salvelinus* family of freshwater fish.

Char are distant relatives of the trout; both families evolved from the same ancestor, *Protothymallus*, which lived 70 million years ago.

Attempts to introduce the American brook trout to British waters have been made since 1869, but with

6. American brook trout

limited success; they seldom if ever breed in the wild in Britain, and have to be artificially reared by fish farms for stocking in suitable waters.

The American brook trout likes to live in cold-water streams and lakes, and has been stocked in some British rivers, streams and still-waters.

The American brook trout has a marble-patterned back, and green-blue sides, dotted with pale yellow-orange and yellow-brown spots.

The behavioural and feeding patterns of the American brook trout are similar to those of the brown trout, and both species can be fished for successfully using much the same methods.

American brook trout in British waters can exceed 2.27kg (5 lb) in weight; though an American brook trout of 1.13kg (2½ lb) in weight should be considered a good size.

Hybrids

Experiments have been made in hybridizing (crossbreeding) brown trout and rainbow trout with American brook trout, to produce two new types of sporting fish.

The resultant hybrids (crossbreeds) are sterile and do not reproduce in the wild.

The American brook trout has been crossbred with the brown trout to produce a fish called the *tiger trout*.

The rainbow trout has been crossbred with the American brook trout to produce the *cheetah trout*.

The tiger trout (American brook trout x brown trout) enjoys a very limited distribution in rivers and still-waters, and where present behaves like a brown trout.

The cheetah trout (American brook trout x rainbow trout) is rarely encountered, and where present behaves like a rainbow trout.

Fish farm trout

Today, many brown trout and almost all rainbow trout in Britain, begin life under artificial conditions in the hatcheries of fish farms.

A *small* fish farm produces about 20 tonnes of trout each year.

Most of the trout reared are marketed commercially as *"table trout"* for cooking and eating: trout of 225g (9 oz) for sale fresh or frozen; trout of 454g (1 lb) for processing; and specially treated pink-fleshed trout of 1.5kg (3 lb 5 oz) and above, for sale as high-priced *"salmon-trout"*.

Fish farm brown trout and rainbow trout, hatched in fresh water, can be *"grown-on"* in floating cages in the *salt water* of the sea, for sale to commercial outlets as *"table trout"*.

Stock fish

Fish farm trout of about 300g (10½ oz) in weight, and of good general appearance and colour, might be selected to *"grow-on"* in fresh water for sale to fisheries for stocking in the flowing waters of rivers and streams, and the still-waters of lakes, reservoirs, pits and ponds.

Trout hatched and raised on fish farms to stock angling waters are known as *stock fish* (commonly called *"stockies"* by anglers).

Stock fish trout are intensively fed in *stew ponds* or floating cages until they reach the desired weight: brown trout are usually considered ready for release at weights of around 0.7kg (1½ lb) and above; rainbow trout may not be released until they weigh 5kg (11 lb) and over!

Fish farm trout are protected and cared for in optimum conditions; they are nourished on high-protein food pellets from alevin stage (see page 21), to the moment of release in their host waters as new stock fish.

Newly stocked brown trout and rainbow trout are tame; see people as protectors and their primary source of food; have little sense of danger, and no learned hunting and feeding skills. Their life can be short.

Stock-fish brown trout and rainbow trout that survive the rigours of stocking, natural predators, and anglers' attempts to capture them, may take 2 years to completely adapt to life in the wild, and even then they will never be truly *wild* trout; though any offspring they produce in the wild will be **wild trout**.

Life-cycle of wild trout
A *wild* trout is a trout which is born, lives and reproduces under natural conditions in the wild.

All wild trout are born in fresh water.

Wild rainbow trout
Rainbow trout are rarely able to reproduce naturally in Britain; only a few waters hold self-sustaining breeding stocks of naturalized wild rainbow trout.

The artificially stocked rainbow trout in most of Britain's waters are unable to shed eggs *(spawn)*, or sperm *(milt)*.

Wild rainbow trout that do breed in Britain usually lay their eggs *(spawn)* between March and May.

The life-cycle of wild rainbow trout is similar to that of wild brown trout.

Wild brown trout
The male *(cock)* brown trout is usually sexually mature at 2–3 years of age; the female *(hen)* brown trout is usually sexually mature at 3–4 years of age.

When brown trout are sexually mature, they are ready

to begin breeding *(spawning)*.

Female brown trout like to lay their eggs *(spawn)* in the clean gravel of clear, oxygen-rich flowing water, where the water temperature is between 40°F (4.4°C) and 55°F (12.8°C).

Trout living in the still-water of lakes and ponds seek out the flowing water of feeder or outflow streams to breed.

In early winter (October/November/December), the female trout blasts a hollow *(redd)* in the gravelbed with powerful sweeps of her tail. As the eggs *(spawn)* are being laid, the male trout fertilizes them with sperm *(milt)*. The fertilized eggs *(spawn)* are then covered with gravel by the female trout.

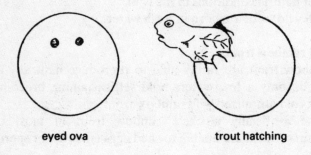

eyed ova   trout hatching

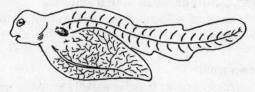

alevin showing yolk sac

7. Birth of a trout

The female trout lays up to 1,500 orange eggs, each egg measuring 6mm (¼ inch) across, in the gravel hollow *(redd)*. Large female trout carrying many eggs may excavate and fill several redds over the space of 2 days, until the female trout is *"spent"* and has no eggs left.

Depending on water temperature, the eggs *(spawn)* may take 3–5 weeks to show signs of life as *eyed ova*, and a further 4–7 weeks to hatch into *alevins*. The alevin (see fig 7, on page 20) is about 25mm (1 inch) long and remains attached to its nourishing yolk-sac for 2–3 weeks before leaving the gravel hollow *(redd)* to seek food.

After 3–6 months the alevin has taken the shape of a tiny young fish *(fry)*. The *fry* grows fast and becomes a *parr* (immature young trout), which has distinctive bluish finger-like markings along its sides.

8. Trout parr

The young trout may remain a *parr* for between 1 and 4 years, depending on the quantity and richness of food available in the water.

Eggs *(spawn)*, alevins, fry and small parr are eaten voraciously by many water creatures, ranging from the underwater larvae of large flies and beetles to minnows and larger fish, including trout.

minnow   water beetle

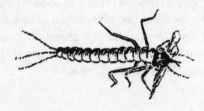

dragonfly larva killing young trout

9. Enemies of young trout

When a brown trout has reached maturity it may develop a silver colour and swim towards the sea. These silver-sided trout are called *smolts* and will become *sea trout* (see page 12), living and feeding at sea, returning to rivers and streams to spawn.

After their first breeding *(spawning)* season, brown trout and sea trout spawn annually in October/November/December.

Male and female brown trout and sea trout that have just completed spawning are called *kelts*. After the effort of spawning the trout are considerably weakened, some die.

Most trout regain peak physical fitness 4–5 months after spawning; depending on the severity of winter and availability of food.

Brown trout normally live for between 6 and 10 years, but can exceed 20 years in age. The large, older trout, turn *cannibal* and live almost exclusively on a diet of small fish. Large cannibal trout seldom waste energy snatching at small flies.

3

THE TROUT'S ANATOMY AND SENSES

Trout are powerful and athletic fish, able to thrive in fast flowing or still-waters.

Trout can live in vigorous water currents flowing at speeds of up to 24.14km (15 miles) per hour.

Trout are streamlined for action.

The trout's body from gills to tail is power-packed muscle.

Trout have supreme eye-body-fin co-ordination.

The trout's mouth is lined with tiny inward-pointing sharp teeth, so prey once seized, can't escape.

TROUT ARE PERFECT PREDATORS.

Anatomy of the trout

All members of the salmon *(Salmonidae)* family can be distinguished by the presence of the fatty, small *adipose* fin on the back, between dorsal fin and caudal fin (tail).

The *dorsal* and *anal* fins enable the trout to balance. The *pectoral* and *pelvic* fins assist movement. The *caudal fin* (tail), combined with body movement, propels the trout through water.

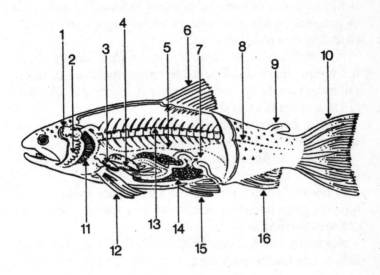

1 brain	9 adipose fin
2 gill rakers	10 caudal fin
3 heart	11 gill filaments
4 liver	12 pectoral fin
5 air bladder	13 vertebrae
6 dorsal fin	14 ovary
7 intestines	15 pelvic or ventral fin
8 lateral line sensor	16 anal fin

10. Anatomy of the trout

The *air bladder* controls air pressure inside the trout, empowering the trout to rise or sink in water and maintain the desired depth.

The *lateral line* is a series of tiny holes (pores), giving the appearance of a line. The pores communicate changes in pressure to the trout's brain, supplying a special sense of *feeling* (see page 29).

An adult trout can swim at 8.05km (5 miles) per hour for hours, reach a comfortable sprint speed of 16.09km (10 miles) per hour, and accelerate to a speed of 24.14km (15 miles) per hour in short bursts.

A hooked trout, racing from an angler for its life, can touch 32.18km (20 miles) per hour.

A wary feeding trout snatches food fast and jets to safety.

A hooked trout's rapid acceleration puts a huge strain on an angler's line. The trout's sudden explosion of energy can break strong line.

An accelerating trout weighing 227g (½ lb) can snap fishing line tested to 1.13kg (2½ lb) breaking strain.

The trout's senses
The trout has highly developed senses of sight, hearing, feeling, smell and taste.

Sight
Trout have *binocular* (focusing with both eyes) vision of what lies before them – to pinpoint prey – and independent *monocular* (one eye only) vision of 180° on each side.

In clear water, trout can see objects up to 4.57m (15 feet) away, and discern different colours; in murky water and at night, trout switch to black and white vision.

Trout have, in effect, all round colour and black and white vision.

The trout's eyes are sensitive to bright light. (Fish have no eyelids to protect their eyes from bright light.) Trout prefer to avoid bright light by diving deep or swimming into shaded areas of water.

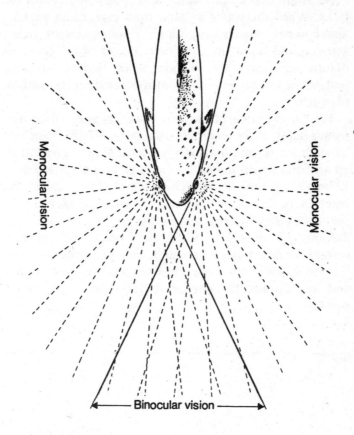

Monocular vision

Monocular vision

←——— Binocular vision ———→

11. The trout's vision

Trout's eyes are slow to adjust to *rapid* changes in light and trout can have trouble focusing when day dawns, suddenly brightens or darkens, or when dusk falls quickly.

AT TIMES OF RAPID CHANGE IN LIGHT TROUT MAY BE SLOW TO SEE US AND WE HAVE AN ADVANTAGE OVER THEM.

Be aware that a *calm water* surface acts as a mirror for trout. When the water is calm, trout can see an angler's above water movements, monitor water surface insect activity, and *simultaneously* view images of below water natural food and the movement of anglers' artificial imitations: images *mirrored downwards* from the surface of calm water.

The trout's area of *surface vision* is affected by the trout's depth in the water. A trout lying 127mm (5 inches) beneath the surface may only see natural prey present, or an artificial fly presented by the angler, in a surface area 127mm (5 inches) across. This area of vision, called the trout's surface *window*, increases in correspondence with the trout's depth beneath the water surface: a trout lying 305mm (12 inches) beneath the surface, will have a surface window vision of about 305mm (12 inches) across. The trout's perception of surface objects becomes dimmer and less distinct the deeper it lies beneath the water surface.

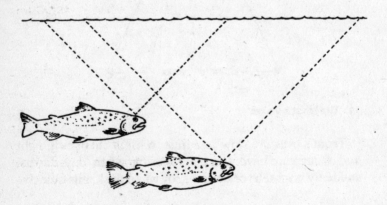

12. The trout's window

A trout intent on surface feeding may not immediately *see* a food item landing outside its surface window area of vision.

ACCURATE CASTING DIRECT TO SURFACE FEEDING TROUT IS VERY IMPORTANT.

Trout have well developed night vision, and, once their sight becomes accustomed to the dark, can locate food by sight.

Trout also employ their other senses.

Hearing

The trout has two sensitive ears inside its head and can hear sound vibrations transmitted through water 12m (40 feet) from the sound's source.

Sound travels 4½ times faster through water (approximately 1 mile or 1.61km per second) than through air. Sound is also clearer in water than in air.

WE MUST APPROACH THE WATERSIDE QUIETLY, TREADING SOFTLY.

Feeling

The trout's *lateral line* (see fig 10, on page 25) of tiny pores along its sides *feels* underwater vibrations (pressure waves), alerting the trout to the presence of objects and minute movements in the water up to 7.62m (25 feet) distant.

Information passed to the trout's brain from the lateral line enables the trout to identify the origin, position, size and speed of the source of the vibrations.

The lateral line helps the trout manoeuvre, detect the slightest change in temperature, and distinguish vibrations that alert the trout to the presence of careless anglers, natural predators, and potential prey.

A *blind* trout can rely on its lateral line to hunt prey, feed and navigate its way around the water. Blind trout turn black in colour, although not all black-coloured trout are blind.

Smell

Trout have a highly developed sense of smell, enabling them to identify minuscule traces of natural scent and track prey for long distances in murky water and at night.

A wary trout will not toy long with an artificial fly impregnated with the telltale smell of human manufacture, storage and handling.

WE MUST BE QUICK TO TIGHTEN OUR LINE AND DRIVE THE HOOK INTO THE MOUTH OF A TROUT INVESTIGATING AN ARTIFICIAL FLY TIED TO OUR FISHING LINE.

Taste

The trout's mouth has sensitive taste buds. Trout are familiar with the normal feel and flavour of their favourite natural foods.

The *unfamiliar* taste and texture of an angler's artificial fly may lead to the artificial's immediate rejection.

The presence of a metal hook will soon be detected and the artificial fly ejected.

WHEN A TROUT INTERCEPTS AND SEIZES OUR ARTIFICIAL FLY, WE HAVE *AT BEST* SECONDS TO ACT BEFORE THE TROUT REALIZES ITS MISTAKE, EJECTS THE FLY AND ESCAPES.

4

THE TROUT'S FOOD

The trout is an extremely active predator, and relies on a high-protein, largely carnivorous (flesh-eating) diet to supply the extraordinary level of energy it expends each day.

A trout's daily food intake may include aquatic flies, insects, larvae, daphnia (water-fleas), shrimps, snails, small fish and frogs; plus any edible morsel that might fall into or be washed into the water, including: earthworms, caterpillars, beetles, slugs, spiders, ants, wasps, bees, craneflies, grasshoppers, berries and small rodents (rats and mice).

The fly-fisher aims to deceive feeding trout into accepting a skilfully presented artificial fly as a *real* insect.

To capture a *wary* trout's interest, the artificial fly should imitate the appearance and motion of a real insect.

To hook the trout, our artificial fly may have to compete successfully with *real* insects already on or in the water.

To be expert fly-fishers, we must first become competent entomologists: learn which insects trout are likely to be feeding on in specific months, and recognize those insects when they are visible on or in the water.

We can then offer feeding trout an artificial fly that

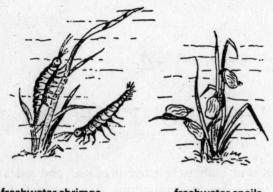

freshwater shrimps   freshwater snails

daphnia (water-flea)   creeper (larva of stonefly)

13. Some aquatic creatures trout eat

closely resembles the insects on which they are dining.

IT PAYS TO HAVE THE RIGHT FLY IN THE RIGHT PLACE AT THE RIGHT TIME.

In Britain, there are four orders of aquatic insects of particular importance to the fly-fisher. Trout eat these aquatic insects avidly at every stage of the insects' development from nymph or larva to adult winged fly: Ephemeroptera ("mayflies"), Trichoptera (sedge-flies), Plecoptera (stoneflies), and Diptera (gnats, midges, etc.).

MAYFLIES
Order: **Ephemeroptera**
The different species of fly belonging to the order *Ephemeroptera,* are commonly called "mayflies".

The mayfly has existed for at least 325 million years. There are over 1,500 different species of mayfly world-wide. The mayfly is found in all continents except Antarctica.

There are about 40 different species of mayfly in Britain.

The largest mayfly in Britain is *Ephemera danica.* The adult mayfly is about 19mm (¾ inch) long, with 16mm (⅝ inch) wingspan and two or three 25mm (1 inch) long tails.

All mayflies of the order *Ephemeroptera* have two large, upright, transparent or opaque wings, and are often referred to by anglers as UPWINGED FLIES.

The life-cycle of the mayfly from fertilized egg to adult consists of four stages:

a) Fertilized egg
b) Nymph
c) Dun (also called sub-imago or sub-adult)
d) Spinner (adult mayfly).

Anglers call dead mayflies *"spent spinners"*.

Ephemeroptera (mayfly)   *Plecoptera* (stonefly)

Trichoptera (sedge-fly)

Diptera (gnat)   *Diptera* (cranefly)

14. Aquatic insects

a) *Beginning stage:* The mated female mayfly lays fertilized eggs on the water.

b) *Underwater stage:* NYMPH
The mayfly nymphs hatch from the fertilized eggs. The nymphal stage normally lasts from 1–2 years. The nymph of *Ephemera danica* grows up to 25mm (1 inch) in length. The nymphs graze on algae and underwater vegetation. In the late spring, summer and autumn months the fully developed nymphs swim to the water surface.

c) *First surface stage:* DUN (also called sub-imago or sub-adult).
The nymph's case splits and the fly emerges to dry its wings.

d) *Second surface stage:* SPINNER (also called *imago* or adult mayfly).
The adult mayflies, wings dried, collect in swarms above the water and mate. The mated females lay their fertilized eggs on the water.

Finally: SPENT SPINNER (dead adult mayfly)
The adult male and female mayflies die soon after mating and egg laying. The life-cycle from emerging *"dun"* to *"spent spinner"* (dead mayfly), is usually over in a few days; during warm weather the cycle is sometimes completed within 24 hours.

Match the hatch – order: *Ephemeroptera*
Artificial nymphs, duns and spinners representing the natural "mayfly" nymphs, duns and spinners of the indigenous UPWINGED "mayfly" species listed here are of particular interest to us.

Autumn Dun *(Ecdyonurus dispar):* Common; found in

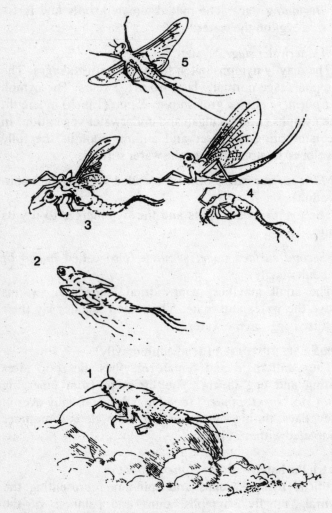

1 mature nymph   **2** swims to surface   **3** emergence
4 dun (sub-imago) sheds nymphal skin   **5** flight

15. The mayfly hatch

still, and flowing waters; favours stony rivers and lakes. Most abundant July–September, when the duns emerge during the DAY.

Blue Winged Olive Dun *(Ephemerella ignita):* Common; found mainly in flowing waters and some still-waters. Most abundant May–October, when the duns emerge during the AFTERNOON/EVENING.

Broadwings *(Caenis & Brachycercus* – six species), also known as Angler's Curse: Common; tiny flies; found in still, and flowing waters. Most abundant June–August, when the duns emerge during the DAY/EVENING.

Claret dun *(Leptophlebia vespertina):* Common; found in still-waters, and occasionally slow-flowing waters. Most abundant May–June, when the duns emerge during the DAY.

Dusky Yellowstreak Dun *(Heptagenia lateralis):* Widespread, not common; found in stony still-waters and stony flowing waters. Most abundant May–September, when the duns emerge during the DAY/EVENING.

Iron Blue Dun *(Baetis niger & Baetis muticus):* Common; found in flowing waters. Most abundant May–October, when the duns emerge during the DAY.

Lake Olive Dun *(Cloeon simile):* Common; found in still, and flowing waters. Most abundant April–June, and again August–October, when the duns emerge during the DAY.

Large Brook Dun *(Ecdyonurus torrentis):* Common; found in stony flowing waters. Most abundant April–July, when the duns emerge during the DAY/EVENING.

Large Dark Olive Dun *(Baetis rhodani):* Common; found in flowing waters. Most abundant February–May; also September–November. The duns emerge during the DAY.

Large Summer Dun *(Siphlonurus lacustris; also Siphlonurus armatus* and *Siphlonurus alternatus):* Localized; found mainly in north-west England, Wales, Scotland, western Ireland, in still, and flowing waters. Most abundant June–August, when the duns emerge during the DAY.

March Brown Dun *(Rithrogena germanica):* Widespread, except southern England, though not common; found in stony flowing waters. Most abundant March–May, when the duns emerge during the AFTERNOON.

Mayfly Dun *(Ephemera danica & Ephemera vulgata):* The mayfly dun *Ephemera danica* is common; found in still, and flowing waters. Most abundant May–June, when the duns emerge during the DAY. The mayfly dun *Ephemera vulgata* is localized; found in still, and slow-flowing waters in the Midlands and southern England. Most abundant May–June, when the duns emerge during the DAY.

Medium Olive Dun *(Baetis vernus & Baetis tenax):* Widespread, though not common, in England and Scotland; found in flowing waters. Most abundant May–October, when the duns emerge during the DAY/EVENING.

Olive Upright Dun *(Rithrogena semicolorata):* Common; found in stony flowing waters. Most abundant May–August, when the duns emerge during the AFTERNOON/

EVENING.

Pale Watery Dun *(Baetis fuscatus):* Common in Wales, north-west and southern England; found in flowing waters. Most abundant May–October, when the duns emerge during the DAY.

Pond Olive Dun *(Cloeon dipterum):* Common; found in still, and flowing waters. Most abundant June–September, when the duns emerge during the DAY.

Sepia Dun *(Leptophlebia marginata):* Widespread, not common; found in still-waters. Most abundant April–May, when the duns emerge during the AFTERNOON.

Small Dark Olive Dun *(Baetis scambus):* Widespread, not common, found in flowing waters. Most abundant June–October, when the duns emerge during the AFTERNOON/EVENING.

Small Spurwing Dun *(Centroptilum luteolum):* Common; found in still, and flowing waters. Most abundant May–September, when the duns emerge during the DAY.

Yellow May Dun *(Heptagenia sulphurea):* Common; found in flowing waters and some still-waters. Most abundant May–August, when the duns emerge during the DAY/EVENING.

SEDGE-FLIES (also known as CADDIS-FLIES)
Order: **Trichoptera**
There are approximately 7,000 species of sedge-fly (called *caddisfly* in North America); about 190 species are known in Britain, most of which are either too small to be of

value to the fly-fisher, or too localized in distribution to be of general interest.

Adult sedge-flies resemble moths, have four hairy wings that fold sloping roof-like back along the body when at rest, and no tails.

Adult sedge-flies live near water and most species are active at night.

The largest sedge-fly in Britain is the Great Red Sedge *(Phryganea grandis)*. The body of an adult Great Red Sedge is about 25mm (1 inch) long, and wingspan 51mm (2 inches).

The antennae of sedge-flies are very long; up to three times the length of the body.

The life-cycle of the sedge-fly from fertilized egg to adult consists of four stages:

a) Fertilized egg
b) Larva (commonly called a *caddis, caddis worm* or *caddis grub*)
c) Pupa
d) Adult

a) *Beginning stage:* The mated sedge-fly lays fertilized eggs on the water or on exposed aquatic plants.

b) *First underwater stage:* LARVA (commonly called a *caddis, caddis worm,* or *caddis grub*).

The sedge-fly larvae hatch from the fertilized eggs. The larvae of most species build a protective open-ended cylindrical case from pieces of plants, sticks, stones, gravel and any other suitable materials found. The protective case is bound together with silk produced from glands on the larva's lower lip.

The case-bearing larva's head and upper body protrude,

and it moves by pulling the case along with its abdomen.

The larva can conceal itself within the case at moments of danger.

The larvae of some species of sedge-fly do not build protective cases; they remain free-living and crawl amongst stones on the waterbed, or construct sheltered lairs – complete with tubes or nets of silk to trap food.

The sedge-fly larvae feed on algae, underwater vegetation and aquatic larvae of other insects.

After about one year, the larva is ready to begin its pupal stage; secures its protective cylindrical case to something solid and seals itself inside.

Larvae that have not built protective cases, construct a cocoon of silk in which to pupate.

c) *Second underwater stage:* PUPA

The pupa takes 2–3 weeks to fully develop *(pupate),* and when ready, bites out of the protective case or cocoon and swims or crawls to the water surface.

d) *Surface stage:* ADULT

At the water surface, the pupa inflates and splits its pupal skin, and emerges as a winged adult sedge-fly.

Adult sedge-flies mate and die within a few weeks.

The entire life-cycle of the sedge-fly is normally completed in just over one year.

Match the hatch – order: *Trichoptera*
Artificial representations of the sedge-fly larva (commonly called *caddis, caddis worm,* or *caddis grub*), sedge-fly pupa and adult sedge-fly of the indigenous sedge-fly species listed here are of particular interest to us.

Black Sedge *(Silo nigricornis):* Common; found on flowing

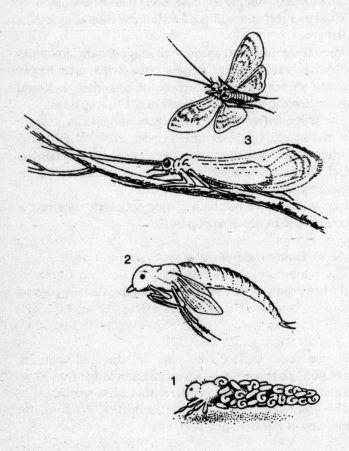

1 sedge larva   **2** sedge pupa   **3** adult sedge-fly

16. Life-cycle of the sedge-fly

waters. Most abundant June–August, when the new adults emerge during the AFTERNOON/EVENING.

Brown Sedge *(Anabolia nervosa):* Common; found on still, and flowing waters. Most abundant June, and again August–September, when the new adults emerge during the EVENING.

Brown Silverhorns *(Athripsodes cinereus):* Widespread; found on still, and slow-flowing waters. Most abundant June–August, when the new adults emerge during the AFTERNOON/EVENING.

Caperer *(Halesus radiatus):* Widespread; found on flowing waters. Most abundant August–October, when the new adults emerge during the AFTERNOON/EVENING.

Cinnamon Sedge *(Limnephilus lunatus):* Common; found on still, and flowing waters. Most abundant June–October, when the new adults emerge during the DAY/EVENING.

Grannom *(Brachycentrus subnubilus):* Widespread; found on flowing waters. Most abundant April–June, when the new adults emerge during the DAY/EVENING.

Great Red Sedge *(Phrygania grandis);* Common; found on still, and flowing waters. Most abundant May–June, when the new adults emerge during the AFTERNOON/EVENING.

Grey Flag *(Hydropsyche instabilis):* Common; found on fast-flowing waters. Most abundant June–July, when the new adults emerge during the DAY/EVENING. The Grey Flag is a DAY-FLYING species.

Grey Sedge *(Odontocerum albicorne):* see **Silver Sedge**.

Grouse-Wing *(Mystacides longicornis):* Common; found on still-waters. Most abundant June–August, when the new adults emerge during the AFTERNOON/EVENING.

Marbled Sedge *(Hydropsyche contubernalis):* Widespread; found on flowing waters. Most abundant June–July, when the new adults emerge during the AFTERNOON/EVENING.

Medium Sedge *(Goera pilosa):* Common; found on still, and flowing waters. Most abundant May–July, when the new adults emerge during the DAY/EVENING. The Medium Sedge is a DAY-FLYING species.

Mottled Sedge *(Glyphotalius pellucidus);* Widespread; found on still-waters. Most abundant May–September, when the new adults emerge during the AFTERNOON/EVENING.

Sand Fly *(Rhyacophila dorsalis):* Common; found on flowing waters. Most abundant April–September, when the new adults emerge during the AFTERNOON/EVENING.

Silver Sedge *(Odontocerum albicorne),* also known as **Grey Sedge**: Widespread; found on fast-flowing waters. Most abundant June–September, when the new adults emerge during the DAY/EVENING.

Small Red Sedge *(Tinodes waeneri):* Common; found on still, and slow-flowing waters. Most abundant May–September, when the new adults emerge during the AFTERNOON/EVENING.

Welshman's Button *(Seriscostoma personatum):* Wide-spread; found on flowing waters and some still-waters. Most abundant June–July, when the new adults emerge during the DAY/EVENING. Welshman's Button is a DAY-FLYING species.

STONEFLIES
Order: **Plecoptera**
There are approximately 1,550 species of stonefly; about 34 species are found in Britain, most of them too rare or localized to be of interest to the fly-fisher.

Adult stoneflies range in size from the Needle Fly *(Leuctra fusca)*, which is about 6mm (¼ inch) long, to the Large Stonefly *(Perla bipunctata),* which grows to just over 25mm (1 inch) in length, with a wingspan of 51mm (2 inches).

Adult stoneflies have four wings that lie flat over the body when at rest, and two tails.

The adult stonefly is a weak and poor flier, spending much of its short life hiding on or near the ground.

Some short-winged species of stonefly are incapable of flight.

The adults of most species of stonefly are found near clean, well-oxygenated fast-flowing stony rivers and streams; some species are found near slow-flowing waters or the rocky shores of large still-waters.

The life-cycle of the stonefly from fertilized egg to adult consists of three stages:

a) Fertilized egg
b) Nymph (nymph of larger species commonly called *creeper*)
c) Adult

a) *Beginning stage:* The mated female stonefly lays fertilized eggs on the water.

b) *Underwater stage:* NYMPH (nymph of larger species commonly called *creeper*).

The stonefly nymphs hatch from the fertilized eggs. The nymphs crawl among the stones of the waterbed and feed on algae and underwater vegetation. Nymphs *(creepers)* of the larger species are voracious predators, seizing and eating small aquatic creatures including worms, sedge-fly pupae *(caddis)*, mayfly nymphs, other stonefly nymphs and small fish-fry.

The nymphal stage can last from 1–4 years, depending on the species. During this time some nymphs shed their skin *(moult)* over 30 times, before the mature nymph finally crawls out of the water onto land.

c) *Surface stage:* ADULT

Once out of the water and on land, the nymph completes its final moult – splitting the nymphal skin to emerge as a winged adult stonefly.

Having lived underwater as a nymph for between 1–4 years, the adult winged stonefly mates and dies within 5 weeks.

NOTE: Because stonefly nymphs *crawl* (don't swim) from the water to land to begin their final moult, artificial representations of the natural stonefly nymph are difficult, though not impossible, for us to present to feeding trout.

Many fly-fishers prefer to concentrate on offering trout an artificial representation of an 'egg laying'' adult female stonefly.

1 nymph   2 adult stonefly

17. Life-cycle of the stonefly

Match the stonefly – order: *Plecoptera*
Artificial representations of the adult female stoneflies of
the indigenous stonefly species listed here are of particular
interest to us.

Large Stonefly *(Perla bipunctata):* Widespread; found on stony flowing waters. Most abundant May–June.

Needle Fly *(Leuctra fusca):* Widespread; found on stony flowing waters and stony still-waters. Most abundant August–October.

Small Brown *(Nemoura cinerea):* Common; found on still-waters and slow-flowing waters. Most abundant March–July.

Small Yellow Sally *(Chloroperla torrentium):* Widespread; found on stony still-waters and stony flowing waters. Most abundant April–July.

Yellow Sally *(Isoperla grammatica):* Widespread; found on stony flowing waters, and shores of rocky large still-waters. Most abundant May–August.

Willow Fly *(Leuctra geniculata):* Widespread; found on stony flowing waters. Most abundant August–October.

GNATS, MIDGES, ETC.
Order: **Diptera**
Some natural flies of special interest to the fly-fisher belong to the order Diptera.

The Diptera order of insects contains more than 85,000 species commonly called flies; over 500 species of Diptera are found in Britain – many have aquatic larvae.

The life-cycle of the different species of fly (order Diptera), which have aquatic larvae, consists of four stages:

a) Fertilized egg
b) Larva
c) Pupa
d) Adult

a) *Fertilized egg*
Mated female lays fertilized eggs on the water.

b) *Larva*
Larvae hatch from the fertilized eggs and live underwater.

c) *Pupa*
Larvae develop and become pupae.

d) *Adult*
Adult flies emerge at the water surface from split pupal skin.

Match the flies – order: *Diptera*
Artificial flies representing the natural adult flies (order: Diptera) listed here are of particular interest to us.

Black Gnat *(Bibio johannis):* Common; found on still, and flowing waters. Most abundant May–September.

Blackfly (Genus: *Simulium*, many species), commonly called "Smut" or "Black Curse": Common; found on flowing waters and large still-waters. Most abundant May–September.

Cranefly (Genus: *Tipula,* many species), also known as **Daddy Longlegs**: Common; found on still, and flowing waters. Most abundant June–September.

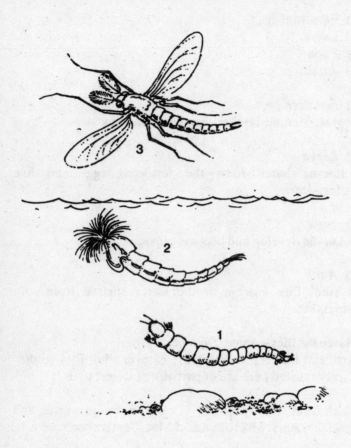

1 midge larva   **2** midge pupa   **3** adult midge

18. Life-cycle of the midge

Hawthorn Fly *(Bibio marci);* also known as **St. Mark's Fly:** Common; found on still, and flowing waters. Most abundant May–September.

Heather Fly *(Bibio pomonae):* Common in Scotland, the north of England, and Wales (also occurs elsewhere – often near heather); found on still, and flowing waters. Most abundant August–September.

Midge (family: *Chironomidae,* numerous species). The non-biting midge species, commonly called *"Buzzers"* are of particular interest to the fly-fisher. Most species are predominantly black, brown or green (some red), in colour; other species are olive, golden-olive, orange-silver in colour. Non-biting midge species are common, and found on still, and flowing waters. Most abundant March–September. The aquatic larvae of non-biting midges are commonly called *"bloodworms"*.

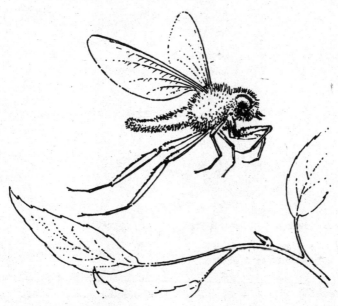

19. Hawthorn fly

OTHER AQUATICS
The natural flies of the orders Ephemeroptera, Trichoptera, Plecoptera, Diptera, and their nymphs, larvae, and pupae are of principal importance to the fly-fisher.

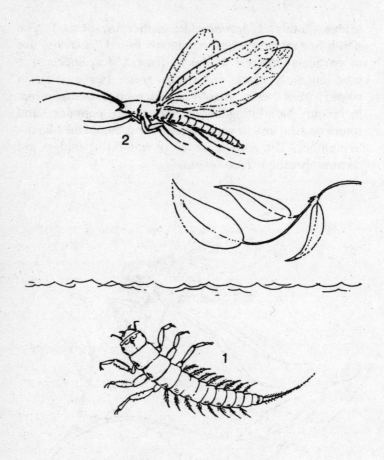

1 larva   2 adult alderfly

20. Life-cycle of the alderfly

Other aquatic creatures of special interest to us, include:

Alderfly larvae, aquatic beetles, cranefly larvae, damselfly nymphs, dragonfly nymphs, small fish (minnows, sticklebacks, etc.), small fish-fry (any species of fish), leeches, freshwater lice, freshwater shrimps, freshwater snails, tadpoles, water-mites.

TERRESTRIALS
Many non-aquatic, land-based *(terrestrial)* creatures hover slightly above, alight on, are blown into, fall into, or are washed into (by rain or flood water), still or flowing waters, and are eagerly snatched by hungry trout.

The terrestrial creatures trout most often encounter on or in the water are of special interest to us, and include:

Alderflies (begin life underwater as *nymphs*), ants, bees, beetles, caterpillars, craneflies (begin life underwater as *larvae*), damselflies (begin life underwater as *nymphs*), dragonflies (begin life underwater as *nymphs*), grasshoppers, moths, sawflies, wasps.

Hungry trout
The trout's healthy appetite *tempts* it to try any food-like item that promises nourishment.

Trout are often ready to sample a new and unfamiliar titbit that presents itself to them in an enticing manner.

The trout's readiness to experiment with new and unfamiliar types of "food" gives us an enormous advantage.

THE SKILFUL PRESENTATION OF ANY ARTIFICIAL FOOD-LIKE ITEM CAN HOOK A HUNGRY TROUT.

Note: **A list of the more successful and popular traditional artificial dry and wet trout-flies begins on page 107.**

5

TACKLE, LINES, KNOTS AND ACCESSORIES

Notes to help you select and assemble the right tackle, line rigs and tackle accessories, for maximum fly-fishing success.

Tackle dealers

Visit your local fishing tackle dealer, view the fly-fishing tackle and accessories on display. Ask the tackle dealer's expert advice on tackle choice, and buy quality items the dealer recommends which you have inspected, like the look and feel of, and are certain will suit your purpose.

Be wise and happy with your choice of fly-fishing tackle and you will be expertly equipped and supremely confident when you begin fly-fishing for trout.

Rods

A fly-fishing rod of about 2.6m (8½ feet) – 2.9m (9½ feet) in length, is ideal for streams, rivers and most fly-fishing on still-waters.

To achieve long distance casts of around 32m (35 yd), sometimes necessary to reach feeding trout on the still-waters of *large* lakes, lochs and reservoirs, a fly-fishing rod of about 2.9m (9½ feet) – 3m (10 feet) in length, may prove a practical choice.

Reel

A fly-fishing reel should be light in weight and of strong construction.

A fly-fishing reel of about 89mm (3½ inches) – 102mm (4 inches) in diameter is ideal for streams, rivers and fly-fishing on still-waters.

Fly-fishing reel spool line capacities vary: for fly-fishing on streams and small rivers, a full reel spool capacity of *at least* 73m (80 yd) backing line and attached fly-line (see page 60) is usually adequate; for fly-fishing on large rivers, and still-waters, a full reel spool capacity of *at least* 96m (105 yd) backing line and attached fly-line (see page 60) is desirable.

A fly-fishing reel with a large line capacity can be used for fly-fishing on rivers, streams and still-waters.

AFTM

Fly-fishing rods and fly-fishing lines carry an AFTM *(Association of Fishing Tackle Manufacturers)* number. The rod's AFTM number indicates the range of fly-line weights the rod has been designed to cast.

The heavier a fly-line, the higher the line's AFTM number.

For optimum line-casting performance, match the recommended AFTM number of the rod and fly-line. For example: a fly-fishing rod with an AFTM line rating of 5–7 (AFTM 5–7), is designed to cast fly-lines of weights numbered AFTM 5, 6, or 7.

A fly-line too light or too heavy for the rod will not cast properly.

AFTM fly-line numbers 1–4 are ideal for fly-fishing on

brooks, becks and burns for small trout.

AFTM fly-line numbers 4–6 are ideal for fly-fishing on streams.

AFTM fly-lines numbers 6 and 7 are suitable for fly-fishing on rivers and most still-waters.

AFTM fly-line numbers 7–9 are suitable for fly-fishing on *large* lakes, lochs and reservoirs, where strong winds blow, and long distance casts of round 32m (35 yd), may sometimes be necessary to reach trout feeding far from the bank or shore.

AFTM fly-line numbers 10–12 are mostly used by fly-fishers pursuing sizeable salmon.

Fly-line tapers

A fly-fishing line is tapered to assist its flight through the air when cast, and enable the fly-fisher to present the artificial fly in the most delicate and natural manner possible to feeding trout.

Double taper (DT)

21. Double taper fly-line

The double taper fly-line is tapered at both ends of its length and can be reversed on your reel spool when one regularly-fished tapered end is reduced through normal cutting, breakage and trimming.

The double taper fly-line is an excellent and economical choice of line where delicate presentation of your artificial fly is desired at close to medium distance on streams, rivers and still-waters.

Weight forward (WF)

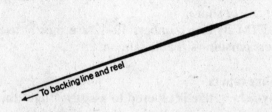

22. Weight forward fly-line

The weight forward fly-line tapers at one end only, and is specially designed to achieve long distance casts on rivers and still-waters.

Shooting head, also called **Shooting taper (ST)**

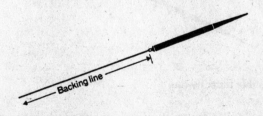

23. Shooting head or shooting taper fly-line

The shooting head or shooting taper fly-line has a tapered head which enables proficient casters to achieve very long distance casts on the still-waters of *large* lakes, lochs and reservoirs.

Floating and sinking fly-lines
In addition to being tapered, fly-lines are manufactured to float on the water surface, or sink through the water at particular speeds.

Floating: designed for use when trout are feeding at the water surface on adult flies emerging, or newly emerged, from their nymphal or pupal skins, egg-laying female flies, or insects alighting on or blown onto the water surface, and struggling to get out of the water; also when trout are feeding just below the water surface on nymphs or pupae; recently drowned flies/insects, etc.

Slow sinking: designed to sink slowly towards a mid-water depth, when trout are feeding avidly on ascending nymphs or pupae, or chasing small fish or fish-fry.

Fast sinking: designed to sink quickly towards trout feeding on or near the water bottom, where the artificial fly will be fished to imitate the natural movements of an insect, aquatic creature, or small fish.

The right rod, reel and lines for beginners
I suggest (it's *your* choice!) the following rod, reel and fly-line combinations to begin fly-fishing on rivers, streams and still-waters:

Fly-fishing rod, AFTM line rating in the range AFTM 5–7, of about 2.6m (8½ feet) – 2.9m (9½ feet) in length; fly-fishing reel of about 89mm (3½ inches) – 102mm

(4 inches) in diameter (see page 56); floating weight forward (WF) AFTM 6 or 7 fly-line, and/or floating double taper (DT) AFTM 6 or 7 fly-line.

Beginners intending to fly-fish for trout on *streams*, will enjoy better sport with a floating double taper (DT) AFTM 5 or 6 fly-line.

Backing line
Fly-lines are about 27.4m (30 yd) in length, and need to be tied to strong *backing line,* which helps fill the fly-fishing reel spool, gives extra line to cast long distances, and allows for occasional line-stripping sprints by especially large trout.

The reel spool should be filled with backing line and attached fly-line, to within about 6mm (¼ inch) of the reel spool's full line capacity (see page 56).

Backing line to reel
Secure the backing line to your reel, using the **reel knot** (see fig 24, below). Ensure the line is tight and evenly wound – loose line can tangle and lead to reel jams.

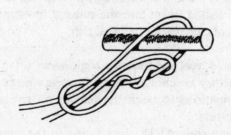

24. Reel knot

Fly-line to backing line
Tie your fly-line to the backing line using either the **needle knot** (see fig 25, on page 62), or the **Albright knot** (see fig 26, on page 62).

Leaders, also called casts
The tapered leader line (also called a *"cast"*), assists to present your artificial fly in the most delicate and "natural" way possible to feeding trout.

A leader line is the tapered link between fly-line and artificial fly.

Your tapered leader line should normally be about 2.7m (9 feet) – 3.3m (11 feet) in length.

Knotless leaders
Commercially manufactured, ready-made *knotless* continuous taper leader lines are marketed and available from your local fishing tackle dealer.

TIP
Follow the manufacturer's instructions and cut the *knotless* continuous taper leader line to achieve the final breaking-strain line strength you require; then tie on an *additional* line of the final breaking-strain strength you require, about 610mm (2 feet) in length, using the **double grinner knot** (see fig 27, on page 64), or the **water knot** (see fig 28, on page 64) or the **blood knot** (see fig 29, on page 64). By tying on the additional line, you avoid having to cut back along the knotless continuous taper leader line whenever you tie on a different artificial fly.

Make your own leaders
You may choose to make your own tapered leader line by knotting lines of different breaking-strain strengths

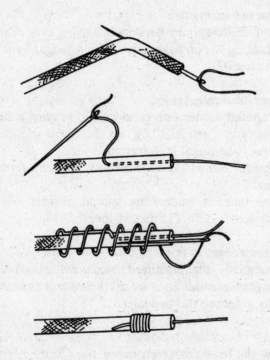

25. Needle knot

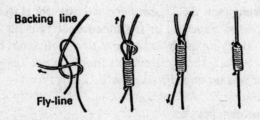

Backing line

Fly-line

26. Albright knot

together to give you a tapered leader line of about 2.7m (9 feet) – 3.3m (11 feet) in length.

Tying a leader

Note: To tie your own tapered leader line, use the **double grinner knot** (see fig 27, on page 64), or the **water knot** (see fig 28, on page 64), or the **blood knot** (see fig 29, on page 64).

A simple example: To make your own tapered leader line of 3m (10 feet) in length, tie 610mm (2 feet) of 9kg (20 lb) breaking-strain line to 610mm (2 feet) of 6.7kg (15 lb) breaking-strain line, tie on 610mm (2 feet) of 4.5kg (10 lb) breaking-strain line, finally tie on 1.2m (4 feet) of 2.7kg (6 lb) breaking-strain line (the *leader point* or *tippet*).

To make a tapered leader line of 2.7m (9 feet) in length, reduce the measurement of each of the four sections by 76mm (3 inches).

To make a tapered leader line of 3.3m (11 feet) in length, increase the measurement of each of the four sections by 76mm (3 inches).

You can step down the leader line knotted sections to a leader point or tippet breaking-strain strength of your choice.

Some fly-fishers tie their leader lines with up to 6 or 7 separate sections of line, each section steadily reducing in breaking-strain strength towards the final 6th or 7th leader point or tippet section.

Leader to fly-line

The thick, high breaking-strain-strength end of your tapered leader line is tied to the fly-line using the **needle knot** (see fig 25, opposite), or the **nail knot** (see fig 30, on page 65).

27. Double grinner knot

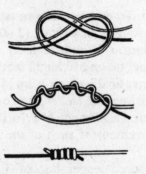

28. Water knot

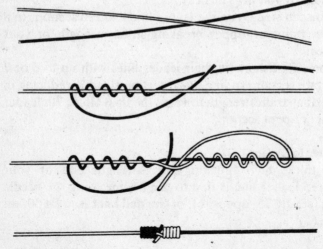

29. Blood knot

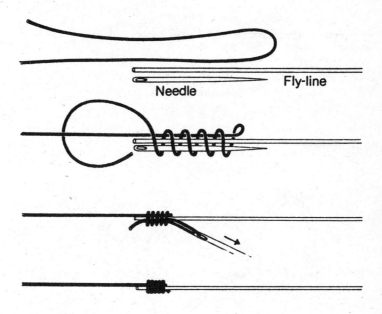

30. Nail knot

Leader point or tippet

The fine, low breaking-strain-strength end section of your tapered leader line is called the **leader point** or **tippet**.

Before fly-fishing, your artificial fly is tied to the leader point or tippet, using the **grinner knot** (see fig 31, on page 66), or **tucked half blood knot** (see fig 32, on page 66).

TO SUM UP: THE BACKING LINE IS TIED TO THE REEL SPOOL, THE FLY-LINE IS TIED TO THE BACKING LINE, THE LEADER LINE IS TIED TO THE FLY-LINE. THE ARTIFICIAL FLY IS TIED TO THE LEADER LINE'S POINT OR TIPPET.

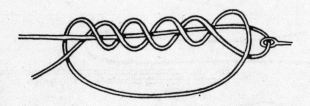

31. Grinner knot

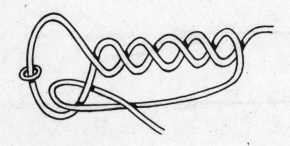

32. Tucked half blood knot

TIP

Should you wish to make swift and easy changes of
complete leader lines, tie a line of about 9kg (20 lb)
breaking-strain, and about 457mm (18 inches) in length,
to your fly-line using the **needle knot** (see fig 25, on
page 62) or the **nail knot** (see fig 30, on page 65). Tie a
loop at the end of the line, using the **loop knot** (see fig 33,
on page 67).

Tie a loop at the thick, high breaking-strain 'butt' end of
your leader line, using the **loop knot** (see fig 33, on

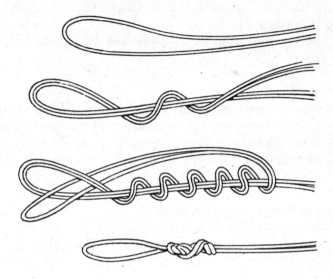

33. Loop knot

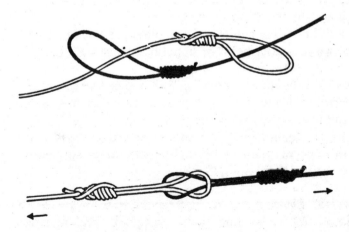

34. To join looped lines

page 67); simply connect the two looped lines as shown in fig 34, on page 67.

Leader lines can be disconnected and replaced in minutes!

TIP

To tighten knots fully, lubricate them with saliva or by dipping them in water before pulling tight. Saliva or water moistens the knot, easing the turns of line together firmly under pressure. Trim the knot loose ends *close* to the knot.

Leader point or tippet strengths

To balance the overall line strength and reduce the risk of a large trout breaking your leader line, match the leader point or tippet breaking-strain strength to the AFTM number of your fly-line.

AFTM fly-line numbers 1–4 should be tied to a leader line with a leader point or tippet breaking-strain strength of about 0.91kg (2 lb) – 1.81kg (4 lb).

AFTM fly-line numbers 5 or 6 should be tied to a leader line with a leader point or tippet breaking-strain strength of about 1.81kg (4 lb) – 2.7kg (6 lb).

AFTM fly-line numbers 7 or 8 should be tied to a leader line with a leader point or tippet breaking-strain strength of about 2.7kg (6 lb) – 3.6kg (8 lb).

AFTM fly-line number 9 should be tied to a leader line with a leader point or tippet breaking-strain strength of about 3.2kg (7 lb) – 4kg (9 lb).

The "X" Scale

Sometimes leader line point or tippet breaking-strain strengths are referred to by an "X" scale.

6X is about 0.91kg (2 lb) breaking-strain.
5X is about 1.4kg (3 lb) breaking-strain.
4X is about 1.8kg (4 lb) breaking-strain.
3X is about 2.3kg (5 lb) breaking-strain.
2X is about 2.7kg (6 lb) breaking-strain.
1X is about 3.6kg (8 lb) breaking-strain.
0X is about 4kg (9 lb) breaking-strain.

Artificial flies

Buy artificial flies expertly tied (*"dressed"*), on best quality *sharp* hooks.

Artificial dry flies are designed to be fished floating on the water surface.

Artificial wet flies, including artificial nymphs, pupae and larvae (also "lures"), are designed to be fished sunk just beneath or well below the water surface.

Weighted artificial nymphs, pupae, larvae and lures, are designed to descend quickly in deep or fast-flowing water.

Ready-made artificial flies are tied or *"dressed"* to various designs or *patterns*. The same artificial fly may be commercially available tied as a dry fly, using a dry-fly pattern, and tied as a wet fly, using a wet-fly pattern.

Lures: some lures resemble small fish or small fish-fry; many lures represent no known aquatic life form.

Lures are fished "wet", and may be presented at all water levels from just beneath to deep below the water surface; skilful *lively* retrieval of the lure attracts, excites and entices trout to snatch the lure.

Lures can be effective, fished wet, at any time of year.

Lures resembling small fish-fry can be especially effective June–October, fished wet on still or flowing waters.

Successful and popular lures, fished mostly on still-waters, **include:** Ace of Spades, Appetiser *(fry)*, Baby Doll, Black Chenille, Dog Nobbler, Jersey Herd *(fry)*, Missionary *(fry)*, Muddler Minnow *(fry)*, Perch Fry *(fry)*, Sweeney Todd, Viva, Whisky Fly.

TIP
Consistently successful "all-round" artificial trout-flies to carry ready for use on flowing or still-waters, **include:** Coachman (dry and wet patterns), Gold Ribbed Hare's Ear "GRHE" (dry and wet patterns), Greenwell's Glory (dry and wet patterns), Grey Duster (dry pattern), Palmer (dry and wet patterns), Pheasant Tail (dry and wet patterns), Wickham's Fancy (dry and wet patterns).

Chapter 11, Traditional Artificial Flies, beginning on page 107, lists some of the more successful and popular traditional dry and wet trout-flies.

Line and fly accessories
Important and useful line and artificial fly accessories, available from your local fishing tackle dealer, **include:**

"Floatants": fly-line grease to make your leader line float; also dry-fly oil, paste or spray to help artificial dry flies float on the water surface.

"Sinkants": commercial preparations to remove grease from your leader line and make the leader line sink.

Cast carriers: spare leader lines can be tied and wound onto circular cast carriers, then stored and carried with you on fly-fishing trips.

TIP
Spare reel spool: often useful; when filled with ready-tied

backing line, fly-line and leader line, makes possible speedy waterside changes of complete fly-fishing line in one swift action.

Fly boxes: essential for safe storage and transporting of your artificial flies. Always dry used artificial flies *before* returning them to their box.

Hook sharpener: to keep the hook point of your artificial flies trout-hooking sharp.

Tackle accessories
Important and useful fly-fishing tackle accessories, available from your local fishing tackle dealer, **include:**

Landing-net: adjustable (telescopic) long-handled large (wide-mouthed) landing-net; essential to land hooked big trout, that threaten to break your leader line.

Artery forceps: to remove the hook from a trout's mouth with speed, and without harm to the trout, should you intend returning the trout to its water.

Scissors: a small pair of *sharp* scissors to snip line and trim loose ends of knots at the waterside.

Priest: weighty blunt instrument to kill trout instantly and humanely (see page 101); called a "priest" because it administers the trout's last rites – an old angling joke!

Marrow spoon: to scoop out the stomach contents of a freshly caught and killed trout, to see what the trout has been feeding on.

Rod bag or rod tube: to store, protect and transport your fly-fishing rod.

Reel case: to store, protect and transport your fly-fishing reel.

Tackle bag: to store, protect and transport your fly-fishing tackle and accessories.

Bass bag: specially designed to carry home your bumper fresh catch of big trout.

Clothing: (refer also to chapter 10 Personal Safety, beginning on page 103). Check you have adequate warm and waterproof clothing. A special fly-fisher's many-pocketed *waistcoat* or *"vest"* supplies handy places to lodge nick-nacks ready for easy access when required.

A *peaked cap* or *floppy hat* and *polarizing sunglasses* provide protection for your eyes and head (see chapter 10); the peaked cap or floppy hat also shades your eyes and together with the polarizing sunglasses, reduces glare from the water, enabling you to see trout ordinarily hidden from view.

Insect repellent: never be without it!

6

CASTING

Casting a fly-line is not difficult. Correctly cast, your rod and line do the work – powering your artificial fly to the precise point you want the artificial fly to reach.

TO BEGIN FLY-FISHING THE RIGHT WAY, TAKE EXPERT CASTING ADVICE AND TUITION FROM A QUALIFIED CASTING INSTRUCTOR.

The best way to learn the right way to cast a fly-line: take invaluable instruction from a qualified casting instructor. A few hours' personal tuition is all you should need to become reasonably proficient in correct and accurate casting of your fly-line.

Angling clubs offering fly-fishing can arrange casting lessons for members; managers of trout fisheries often organize casting tuition: fishing tackle dealers can usually recommend local qualified casting instructors who give tuition; some local councils offer courses in fly-line casting, and qualified casting instructors advertise their services in local newspapers, angling newspapers and angling magazines.

The right hold
The right hold for a fly-fishing rod – comfortable and firm,

see fig 35, below.

35. The right hold for a fly rod

The overhead cast

The overhead cast is the basic fly-fishing cast to master.

Look round to check all is clear – no trees, shrubs, bushes **or people**. Stand comfortably. Strip and loop a metre or more of fly-line from your reel, see fig 36, on page 75.

36. Preparing to cast

Using your forearm and with a final flick of the wrist, bring your rod vertically upright so the length of line at the rod tip straightens out behind – parallel to the ground, bending the rod tip. This is called the **back cast**, see page 76, fig 37 (i). Then bring the rod forwards, in the **forward cast**, see page 76, fig 37 (ii). If the line cracks like a whip, you have brought the line forwards too soon – before the line was fully extended behind you. Release the looped fly-line held in your free hand. When the position shown in fig 37 (iii) is reached, the downwards movement of your rod is halted and the artificial fly alights gently on the water.

TIMING AND RHYTHM COME WITH PRACTICE.

37. The cast in progress

Shooting the line

To cast a long distance – "shoot your line".

Hold several metres of fly-line looped in your free hand. Make the overhead cast, and just as the pull of the line exerts pressure on the rod tip, release the looped fly-line held in your free hand.

When you have become fully proficient in the overhead cast and shooting the line, there are other useful casting techniques to learn, including "double haul", which enables you to cast your fly-line very long distances.

Meanwhile, **practice** helps make perfect!

Advice

Though it may seem obvious advice, do not become *obsessed* with casting your fly-line simply for the sake of casting.

If you can crawl close to a trout feeding near the bank or shore, or stealthily approach a likely trout-holding location, and skilfully present your artificial fly without casting your fly-line, do so!

And remember these words of wisdom:

YOU CATCH MORE TROUT WHEN YOUR ARTIFICIAL FLY IS ON OR IN THE WATER THAN WHEN THE FLY IS IN THE AIR.

7

FLY-FISHING METHODS

DRY-FLY FISHING
Dry-fly fishing is the skilful art of presenting an artificial fly on the water surface in imitation of a natural insect.

A *dry* fly is an artificial fly which is designed to be "fished dry", floating on the water surface.

Fishing the dry fly is a most effective and thrilling way to catch trout rising to snatch natural flies at the water surface.

Fishing the rise
The aim of *"fishing the rise"*, is to locate a surface-feeding ("rising") trout and skilfully present the trout with an artificial dry fly which imitates the appearance and motion of the real flies upon which the trout is feeding.

IF YOU DO NOT HAVE THE RIGHT ARTIFICIAL DRY FLY TO MATCH THE NATURAL FLIES ON THE WATER, OFFER A DRY FLY OF SIMILAR SIZE AND COLOUR (MATCHING THE SIZE IS MORE IMPORTANT THAN MATCHING THE COLOUR).

Fishing the water
When you cannot see trout rising to feed at the water surface, try *"fishing the water"*: cast your fly-line to

present the artificial dry fly on areas of water where you expect trout to be lying (see chapter 8, Locating Trout, beginning on page 86).

A TROUT MAY BE LYING JUST BENEATH THE WATER SURFACE.

A hungry or inquisitive trout may journey from the water bottom to intercept an artificial dry fly presented enticingly on the water surface.

Fishing the water can produce excellent sport.

Tackle notes (see also chapter 5, beginning on page 55).
Fly-fishing tackle suitable for dry-fly fishing on rivers, streams and still-waters.

Suitable rods (see page 55), fly-fishing rod; about 2.6m (8½ feet) – 2.9m (9½ feet) in length, AFTM line rating in the range AFTM 5–7. For *large* still-waters, where long distance casts of round 32m (35 yd) may sometimes be necessary, a fly-fishing rod of about 2.9m (9½ feet) – 3m (10 feet) in length, AFTM line rating 7–9, may prove a practical choice.

Suitable reels (see page 56), fly-fishing reel; 89mm (3½ inches) – 102mm (4 inches) in diameter.

Suitable fly-lines (see page 57), include: floating double taper (DT), AFTM 5–7; floating weight forward (WF), AFTM 5–7. For *large* still waters: floating double taper (DT), AFTM 7–9; floating weight forward (WF), AFTM 7–9.

Suitable leader point or tippet breaking-strain strengths (see page 68): 0.91kg (2 lb) – 4kg (9 lb).

Suitable artificial flies: Dry flies (see list beginning on page 107); hook sizes: (large) 8/10/12/14/16 (small).

Line and fly accessories: "Floatants" (see page 70), fly-line grease to make your leader line float, and dry-fly oil, paste or spray to help your artificial dry fly float on the water surface.

Rivers and streams – dry-fly methods
Upstream casting

Approach a rising trout from downstream *(down current)*. Trout living in rivers and streams face upstream *(up current)* – into the water current, and are unaware of a *stealthy* angler's cautious approach. Cast your fly-line upstream *(up current)*, to place the artificial dry fly about 152mm (6 inches) – 457mm (18 inches), and not more than 610mm (2 feet), in front of the surface-feeding trout; let the water current carry your artificial dry fly towards the trout.

Downstream casting

Casting your fly-line downstream *(down current)*, towards a surface-feeding trout – which will be facing towards you – is sometimes the only practical way to present an artificial dry fly to a trout rising in an area of water not easily accessible for an orthodox upstream *(up current)* cast.

A downstream *(down current)* cast can be made to inaccessible areas of water likely to hold trout when *"fishing the water"*, to attract the attention of any unseen trout lying beneath the water surface, or at the water bottom.

Cross-country casting

To present your artificial dry fly to a surface-feeding trout lying near the bank from which you are fishing, or to an area of water close to the bank likely to hold a trout, move quietly to a position directly opposite the rising trout or promising area of water; stand well back from the water – beyond the trout's view; cast your fly-line above and across the bank to place your artificial dry fly just upstream *(up current)* from your target area, and let the water current carry your artificial dry fly to the point you want it to reach.

Still-water – dry-fly methods

Approach the water with stealth and look for signs of trout rising to feed at the water surface. Cast directly to a surface-feeding trout. Aim to place your artificial dry fly about 152mm (6 inches) – 457mm (18 inches), and not more than 610mm (2 feet), in front of the surface-feeding trout; if the trout is slowly feeding its way *across* the water surface, cast your fly-line ahead of the trout, in the direction the trout appears to be heading. Give the line an occasional slight jerk to "twitch" the artificial dry fly into attractive lifelike motion.

When there are no visible signs of trout rising to feed at the water surface, cast your fly-line to a favourable-looking location (see chapter 8, Locating Trout, beginning on page 86).

Permit the artificial dry-fly time to settle, then retrieve the line slowly, with occasional slight jerks to impart trout-attracting, lifelike movement to the artificial dry fly. Allow a few seconds for the artificial dry fly to settle in each new position before retrieving more line. Continue retrieval until you have recovered all the line, then cast again.

Continue casting and retrieving your fly-line until you have thoroughly covered and explored the promising area of water before you, then move along to the next propitious place and begin again.

WET-FLY FISHING

A *wet* fly is an artificial fly which is designed to be "fished wet", sunk below the water surface.

Fishing the wet fly is a challenging and rewarding way to catch big trout feeding just beneath or well below the water surface, on recently drowned natural flies, nymphs, pupae, larvae, fish-fry, small fish, and other aquatic creatures.

Successful wet-fly fishing demands high levels of skill and patience; the biggest trout are invariably caught using wet-fly techniques.

The aim of wet-fly fishing is methodically to cover areas of water likely to hold large trout. Cast your fly-line to explore every location where a feeding trout can be seen or *ought* to be lying (see chapter 8, Locating Trout, beginning on page 86).

Persist with your casting and line retrieval until you hook the trout, or are satisfied there is no feeding trout present. Then move along to another promising patch of water and again begin casting and retrieving your fly-line.

Tackle notes (see also chapter 5, beginning on page 55).

Fly-fishing tackle suitable for wet-fly fishing on rivers, streams and still-waters.

Suitable rods (see page 55), fly-fishing rod; about 2.6m (8½ feet) – 2.9m (9½ feet) in length; AFTM line rating in the range AFTM 5–7. For *large* still-waters, where long distance casts of round 32m (35 yd) may sometimes be necessary, a fly-fishing rod of about 2.9m (9½ feet) – 3m (10 feet) in length; AFTM line rating 7–9, may prove a practical choice.

Suitable reels (see page 56), fly-fishing reel; 89mm (3½ inches) – 102mm (4 inches) in diameter.

Suitable fly-lines (see page 57), floating fly-lines suitable for dry-fly fishing (see page 79) can be used: remove grease from the *leader line* with a "sinkant" (see page 70) to make the leader line sink below the water surface.

You can control the depth to which your leader line sinks by using a "floatant" (see page 70) to grease the length of leader line you wish to float on the water surface, and applying a "sinkant" (see page 70) to remove grease from the length of leader line you want to sink below the water surface. This enables you to present your wet fly at depths ranging from just beneath the water surface, to a depth equivalent to the entire length of your leader line.

Suitable wet-fly only fly-lines (see page 59), include: slow sink double taper (DT), AFTM 5–7; slow sink weight forward (WF), AFTM 5–7; fast sink double taper (DT), AFTM 5–7; fast sink weight forward (WF), AFTM 5–7.

For *large* still-waters: slow sink double taper (DT), AFTM 7–9; slow sink weight forward (WF), AFTM 7–9; fast sink double taper (DT), AFTM 7–9; fast sink weight forward (WF), AFTM 7–9; fast sink shooting head or shooting taper (ST), AFTM 7–9.

Suitable leader point or tippet breaking-strain strengths (see page 68): 0.91kg (2 lb) – 4kg (9 lb).

Suitable artificial flies: Wet flies (see list beginning on page

107); also artificial nymphs, pupae, larvae, and lures (see page 69). Suitable wet-fly hook sizes: (large) 8/10/12/14/16 (small).

Line accessories: "Sinkants" (see page 70), to remove grease from your leader line and make the leader line sink; also "floatants" (see page 70), when wet-fly fishing with a floating fly-line (see *"Suitable fly-lines"*, beginning on page 83).

Rivers and streams – wet-fly methods
Upstream wet-fly fishing
Approach a visible trout or likely trout-holding location from downstream *(down current)*; cast your fly-line upstream *(up current)*, ahead of the point you wish the sunken wet-fly to reach, casting sufficient fly-line to allow the extra line needed for the wet-fly to sink to its target position. Collect slack line in your hand as the current carries the fly-line back towards you; keep your rod tip raised high and tighten the line to hook your trout the moment you feel a trout-taking tremor transmitted through the fly-line from your wet-fly.

Downstream wet-fly fishing
Cast your fly-line downstream *(down current)*, so the artificial wet-fly is carried downstream and away from you by the current. The taut fly-line will arc across the current and swing back towards the bankside from which you are fly-fishing; retrieve the line with a series of short jerks to impart attractive, lifelike movement to the wet-fly. When you have recovered all the line, cast again. Work your way steadily and methodically downstream *(down current)*.

Downstream wet-fly fishing is sometimes the best way to reach otherwise unresponsive trout lurking at the water's bottom, and is a useful technique when night fishing for trout, particularly sea trout – a wide area of water can be searched with a series of "blind" casts.

Still-water – wet-fly methods

Approach the water quietly and look for signs of trout feeding just beneath or below the water surface (see chapter 8, Locating Trout, beginning on page 86, especially "rise forms", beginning on page 95). Cast your fly-line to reach the position where you can see trout are feeding just beneath or below the water surface. Retrieve the line slowly, with occasional jerks to give your wet-fly lifelike movement. Allow the wet-fly to settle for a few moments in each new position before continuing line retrieval. Continue casting and retrieving your fly-line until satisfied the trout have ceased feeding or moved to another spot.

When there are no visible signs of trout feeding just beneath or below the water surface, choose a location likely to hold or attract feeding trout (see chapter 8, Locating Trout, beginning on page 86) and cast your fly-line to that location.

For maximum chances of success, allow time for your wet-fly to reach a slightly different depth with each cast before retrieving your line, and vary the speed of line retrieval.

Continue casting and retrieving your fly-line until you have thoroughly explored the water with your wet-fly before moving elsewhere.

A TROUT MAY FOLLOW YOUR ARTIFICIAL WET-FLY UNTIL THE MOMENT YOU BEGIN LIFTING IT FROM THE WATER, BEFORE MOVING TO SNATCH THE "ESCAPING" ARTIFICIAL WET-FLY.

8

LOCATING TROUT

Where to locate trout in rivers or streams
Notes to help you locate places in rivers or streams where trout may be lying.

- Beneath overhanging trees or shrubs.
- Near submerged tree roots.
- Near water plants and weed-beds.
- In streamy runs of fast water between weed-beds.
- In steady glides of water between rocks or boulders.
- Inside bends on streams or riverbanks, where food is deposited by the current.
- Where inflowing trickles, rivulets or streams of water drain or flow into the main body of water.
- Where swirling and circling eddies of water draw and trap food from the main current.
- Where a rapid flow of water meets calm or shallow water.
- Alongside and behind boulders that break the current and give trout a sheltered spot from which to seize passing prey.
- In shallow bankside runs, sheltered from strong currents, where insects breed and fish fry cavort.
- In deep, oxygen-rich pools of water below weirs or

waterfalls, and the streamy runs of water near weirs or waterfalls.

● In deep scoured bankside undercuts, where shallow fast water has eaten down into the bank and waterbed, slowing into a deep, lazy, sleeve-shaped run.

● In deep pools of slow moving water.

● In deep holes or hollows in the stream or river bed.

● In deep stretches of smooth-flowing water – trout often lie close to the bank.

● Where two flowing waters, rivers or streams meet and merge in a confusion of currents.

● Beneath bridges, where trout feel secure; especially old stone bridges, whose small cracks and crevices are home to teeming insects that regularly "plop" into the water.

● In rivers or streams with rising water levels (due to rain, or the incoming *flood tide* in tidal waters) – trout feed with enthusiasm, as they also do when the water approaches its *"normal"* level, after flood or drought.

● Close to the bank in rivers or streams in flood – trout move close to the bank to escape strong currents and feed on insects washed into the water.

● Where large chunks of bankside have newly collapsed into the water – trout are attracted to the area by wriggling insects washed from the mud.

● In pools and stretches of water hidden from view by trees, shrubs and dense undergrowth. These areas of water are seldom fished and often hide big trout.

● Any place where you have caught a big trout before – a captured big trout's vacant favourite spot is soon occupied by another large trout!

TIP

Trout queue according to size for food in the best feeding spots. The biggest trout always takes top place. Find ace

38. Haunts of big trout

feeding spots and catch the biggest trout first, then the smaller ones.

TIP
Big trout usually lie in deep water *("pools")*, during the day, and move into shallow water at night to feed.

Where to locate trout in still-waters
Notes to help you locate places in still-waters where trout may be feeding.

● Near water plants and weed-beds.
● Beneath overhanging trees or shrubs.
● Near submerged tree roots.
● Near sunken rocks or boulders.
● In comparatively "shallow" areas of water where aquatic insects breed.
● In deep water bordering shallow areas where aquatic insects hatch and fish fry shoal.
● In deep water near the mouth of inflowing rivers or streams.
● In bays and by promontories (where trout shelter and wait to seize insects blown into the water from the land; insects alighting on the water, etc.).
● In deep, overshadowed (shaded) areas of water.
● In streamy and fast water sweeping past rocky head-lands on large still-water lakes or lochs.
● In channels around small islands, especially any deep holes or gullies and patches of water beneath island tree-branches or bushy shrubs.
● In heavy reed/weed areas, hollows, deep holes and channels near the shore – all examples of locations occupied by big trout waiting to ambush passing prey.
● Where wind-caused currents and cross-currents carry

39. Favourite trout lies in rivers

1 deep shady pools   2 near sunken rocks   3 deep pool   4 rocky stream

particles of food to queuing trout; cast into the current.

● Where rippling wind-driven water meets calm stretches of water protected by bank or shore contours and/or vegetation – food is trapped and whirled to waiting trout. Cast to that point and continue casting methodically along the line of rippling water.

● In deep water near newly collapsed chunks of bankside.

Other pointers

● Scout for patches of bank or shore scoured or worn bare by anglers' boots. Popular places may have much to recommend them, though not always.

● Search for stretches of water hidden from view by trees, bushes and dense growth. These areas of water are seldom fished and often hide big trout.

● Strong gusty winds or squalls drive trout deep in the water, or into sheltered bays. Look for quiet, wind-protected spots, which may offer good sport.

● On sunny summer days, trout feed in stretches of water shaded from strong sunlight. In the evening, the western side of the water will be favoured by trout because it is the first to fall into shadow.

● On windy days fly-fish with the wind blowing from behind you. Trout gather near shallows to feast on insects blown from land into the water. When the wind has ceased, try the opposite bank or shore for bonus catches.

● During cold or changeable weather, expect trout to feed mostly beneath the water surface in deep water, away from the shore. Freezing winter weather may force big trout well down from the water surface.

● During warm weather, trout feed mostly in the upper water level; at the water's surface, and water's edge shallows.

● Check if a detailed map of the water you intend fly-

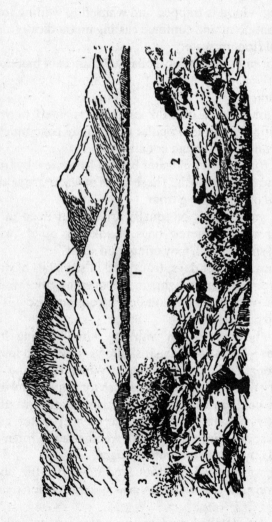

1 deep overshadowed water   2 off rocky headlands   3 near inflowing streams

40. Where trout feed in lakes or lochs

fishing is marketed by the water company/owner, and buy one. The information marked shows obvious "hotspots", and the map is convenient for recording your own secret finds.

● Although trout in still-waters rove widely in search of food, individual brown trout *(Salmo trutta)*, and shoals of rainbow trout *(Salmo gairdneri)*, still have favourite feeding spots, and sometimes become slaves to habit. Careful observation can suggest suitable timing for a shrewdly calculated catch.

● Still-water big trout generally like to have their main meals at dawn, dusk and into the night. At these times they feel safe and are therefore most vulnerable.

Nature's signposts

Let nature signpost the best locations for you to fly-fish for feeding trout.

Look and listen for these signs:

● Rush of small fish (minnows, sticklebacks, etc.), and/or fish fry scattering for cover in shallow water.

● Sudden splashes, ripples, waves or spreading rings on the water surface.

● Watch for kingfishers and herons. They know where small fish are. Big trout won't be far away.

● Birds (swifts, swallows, martins, etc.), snatching insects over the water show you where flies are hatching. Trout will be there too.

● Clouds or swarms of winged-insects above the water.

TIP

Binoculars or a telescope help you spy insect activity and trout-betraying water surface disturbance on large still or flowing waters.

41. The swallow – one of nature's signposts

TIP

Take lessons from the way a heron catches fish: remain as
inconspicuous and quiet as possible when fly-fishing at or

near the water's edge (or afloat in a boat); reduce movement to a necessary minimum; when a trout takes your artificial fly, act immediately with speed and decisiveness to hook and land the trout.

BE PATIENT AND PERSISTENT TO SUCCEED.

Rise forms

To locate feeding trout, watch and listen carefully; there are sometimes clear signals in the water – *"rise forms"* – that tell us where trout are feeding and give clues about what natural food the trout are seeking.

The most important rise forms to look for are:

Surface-breaking *"slashing"* rise

The trout, at speed, breaks the water surface with an audible splash, and may actually twist or leap through the air just above the water surface. The trout is probably snatching at large, fast-moving flies on the water surface – newly emerged or egg-laying sedge-flies; possibly the large mayfly *(Ephemera danica)*; or pursuing a large insect alighting on, flying just above, or blown onto the water surface and struggling to get out of the water: cranefly, dragonfly, hawthorn fly, moth, beetle, grasshopper, etc.

Standard surface *"nosing"* rise

Watch for the trout's nose or head breaking the water surface, followed by outwardly spreading concentric rings of water. The trout is feeding at the water surface on surface hatching insects; adult flies emerging, or newly emerged, from their nymphal or pupal skins. The "nosing" rise is a trout's usual rise for taking duns of a "mayfly" species (order: *Ephemeroptera*).

The surface *"kiss-sip"* rise

The trout's open mouth appears to kiss and sip at the water surface; there is the barest telltale ripple of water. Sometimes you can hear the soft "smacking-kiss" sound. The trout is lying just below the water surface and probably feeding on nymphs or pupae floating slightly below the water surface; recently drowned flies/insects; flies emerging from their nymphal or pupal skins; small adult flies newly emerged from their nymphal or pupal skins; and/or small flies/insects alighting on the water surface.

The surface *"head-and-tail"* rise

The trout – head, back, then tail – rolls gracefully out of the water as it descends on an item of food. The trout is probably feeding at, and slightly below, the water surface on surface-bound nymphs or pupae, recently drowned flies, emerging, and newly emerged adult flies unable to take flight.

The underwater *"sub-surface"* boil

The water surface swirls or whirls and appears to hump, bulge or "boil" as the feeding trout, maybe 457mm (18 inches) – 1.52m (5 feet), beneath the surface, twists, turns and rolls to take ascending nymphs, pupae, etc.

Near surface *"bow-waving"* rise

Trout chasing fish-fry near the water surface, or herding shoals of fry into shallow areas of water where they can trap and eat them in large numbers, produce fast-moving V-shaped "bow-waves". On still-waters, several trout may be herding the fry, usually into shallow water near the bankside or shore. You may see the water surface erupt, as terrified fry scatter for safety.

The "bow-wave" rise is most commonly seen July–October, when feeding trout pay special attention to shoals of well-developed fish-fry.

Weather to locate trout

Trout have to eat to live, and a hungry or inquisitive trout can be tempted to take a skilfully presented artificial fly whatever the weather conditions.

Here is a short list of observations about the way the weather may affect trout living in still or flowing waters.

● A spell of settled weather, when the water is at its "normal" level, suits trout best; they feed steadily and good sport is practically guaranteed.

● A sharp rise in water temperature makes trout especially active; they feed voraciously. If the water temperature exceeds 70°F (21°C), brown trout *(Salmo trutta)*, become torpid and reduce feeding.

Brown trout *(Salmo trutta)*, are most active when the water temperature is 45°F (7.2°C) – 60°F (15.5°C).

Rainbow trout *(Salmo gairdneri)*, are most active when the water temperature is 60°F (15.5°C) – 75°F (24°C).

A sharp drop in water temperature makes trout less active. When the water temperature drops below 40°F (4.4°C), trout reduce feeding.

● Big trout in all waters keep well under the surface in very hot or very cold weather. To catch them, fly-fish shaded areas of deep water.

● On hot summer days trout often feed fast and furiously early morning (dawn) and late evening (sunset). Big trout may start feeding near sunset and continue into the night.

● Wind and rain after a scorching near-drought period can revive and excite trout into a bout of frenzied near-surface and surface feeding.

● On bright, cloudless days, trout feed mainly in deep water.

● On dull, cloudy days, trout will hunt food in shallow water.

● On a dull overcast day, a brief burst of sunshine sometimes brings on a "hatch" of flies, which starts trout rising to feed at the water surface.

● Trout are excited by rain (which raises the oxygen content of the water), and often feed at or near the water surface shortly before, during and after rainfall.

● Heavy rain washes airborne and terrestrial insects/ creatures into the water. Trout gobble them live at the water surface, and drowned just beneath the surface.

● A sudden shower of heavy rain or hail sometimes brings on a "hatch" of flies, which starts trout rising to feed at the water surface.

When *very* heavy rain or hail teems into the water, trout may wait well below the surface, until the rain or hail eases.

● When a wind blows from the west or south, trout are often active near the water surface. Good catches are likely when there is a steady south-westerly breeze on a dull day. When a wind blows from the east or north, trout often stay well down in the water.

● Big trout feed steadily on moonless, mild nights, which can yield fine catches.

9

PLAYING A TROUT

Having enticed a trout to take your skilfully presented artificial fly (nymph, pupa, larva or lure), the next step is to set your hook firm in the trout's mouth, and "play" the trout into your landing-net.

To detect a take and hook the trout
Keep line taut as possible between artificial fly and rod tip; do not permit loose line to wander unchecked across or through the water. Once the trout has tasted your artificial fly, it will soon be spat out. You have not a moment to waste. Look for a trout snatching or nonchalantly taking in its mouth, an artificial fly fished on or slightly below the water surface; *at all times*, feel the taut line for tugs or tremors; watch line on the water for sudden movement – curling, running, straightening, etc. – or an unexpected stop in motion. In all cases *immediately* tighten the line (hold the line near your reel firmly with one hand, and smartly raise the rod tip with your rod-holding hand), and hook your trout.

Aim to get the hooked trout out of the water and into your landing-net quick as possible.

EVERY SECOND A HOOKED TROUT STAYS IN THE WATER GIVES

IT A CHANCE TO ESCAPE.

A powerful trout, fighting for its life, will use every trout-cunning trick it knows to dislodge the hook or break your line. A hooked trout may rocket straight towards line-tangling underwater cover: weed-beds, tree roots, submerged tree trunk, rocks or boulders, etc.

Always work out where a hooked trout is likely to race *before* fly-fishing, and steer the hooked trout from the safety of line-snapping underwater snags.

A hooked trout may leap from the water in an attempt to dislodge the hook, thrash your line with its body and tail, then dive deep into the water to further stretch and strain the line, and test your knots.

I've seen trout shed the hook and leap from a landing-net to water bottom safety.

To play a hooked trout

Keep your rod upright and line taut – a taut line seldom tangles on underwater snags; apply as much pressure on the racing trout as you dare – timid playing loses trout. A particularly powerful and pugnacious trout may be made to yield by applying side-strain (hold your rod parallel to the water surface; side-strain pulls the hooked trout's head from the side and puts the trout off balance). Pump the trout towards you, by reeling-in line while lowering the rod tip, then raise the rod tip and keep the recovered line on your reel. Never give out line unless judged absolutely necessary to avoid breakage.

Defeat a leaping trout's attempt to strain and snap the line by momentarily lowering your rod tip to reduce line tension.

On the flowing waters of rivers or streams, keep downstream *(down current)* of the hooked trout, then the trout can't use the strength of the water's current in its fight against you, and by turning the trout and pulling it downstream *(down current)*, you force the trout's gills shut and it has difficulty breathing. The trout's capacity to fight is reduced.

To land a hooked trout
Steer the hooked trout through the water towards the wide *mouth* of your long-handled landing-net (the mouth of the net should be submerged just below the water surface). When the trout is above the submerged mouth of the landing-net, raise the net and land your trout.

Wet your hands before touching the trout to remove the hook from its mouth. Dry fingers may damage the trout's tiny protective scales, leading to infection if the trout, not wanted for eating, is gently released back into its watery home.

To return a trout caught from the flowing waters of rivers or streams, carefully lower the unhooked trout back into the water facing upstream *(up current)* into the water current, and gently hold the trout steady until it feels strong enough to swim away.

Should you wish to take the captured trout home to make a meal of it, kill the trout quickly and humanely by striking it heavily across the base of its head with a weighty blunt instrument (a "priest", see page 71, is an ideal weapon).

I have seen trout squirm free and leap from the hands of fly-fishers preparing to kill them, back into the water, or thrash their way over the bank or shore or out of a boat and back into the water.

A TROUT NEVER SURRENDERS, IT NEVER GIVES IN.

TIP

Kill trout you want to keep and eat while the trout is in the landing-net, *before* removing the hook from its mouth.

10

PERSONAL SAFETY

Stay safe at the waterside or afloat in a boat, by following these basic guidelines.

Take a friend
Take a friend fly-fishing. Apart from the cheering company, if one of you has an accident, the other can assist or go for help.

Learn to swim
All anglers should be proficient swimmers. Under qualified supervision, learn to swim *at least* 50m (55 yd), fully clothed.

Never go afloat in a boat until you can swim at least 50m (55 yd), fully clothed.

Should you decide to go afloat in a boat in pursuit of trout, always fly-fish with an experienced boat-handler; never fly-fish from a boat on your own – tell someone ashore when to expect your return; wear a life-jacket at all times, and never stand up in the boat, you could capsize the boat and/or fall into the water.

Never wear waders or fishermen's thigh boots in a boat – if you fall overboard, they will quickly fill with water and sink you like a stone!

High-voltage overhead electricity cables

Keep well away from high-voltage overhead electricity cables. A back-cast fishing-line tangle with an overhead cable conducting electricity could kill you. Some cables are surprisingly close to the ground.

Be aware that electricity from an overhead cable can arc down and strike your fishing rod even if you have no direct fishing-line contact with the cable.

Thunderstorms

Do not fly-fish during a thunderstorm.

Lightning can kill.

A strike by lightning could kill you.

Find a safe place to shelter **before** the thunderstorm begins *(breaks)*.

Do not go out in a boat if a thunderstorm is forecast.

If you are afloat in a boat, aim to get ashore before the thunderstorm begins *(breaks)*, and seek a safe place to shelter.

Do not shelter directly beneath a tree, lightning striking the tree could kill you.

Lightning does not always strike the highest point in the area where it flashes to earth. Lightning can strike anywhere.

When caught in the open during an overhead thunderstorm, put your fishing rod, landing-net, and any large metal objects you might be wearing or carrying (lightning is attracted to metal) in a neat pile; move well away from the pile and keep a low profile – kneel, or lie down flat on the ground, and remain in that position until the thunderstorm has passed.

You may get wet and muddy and think you look silly, but you will be alive!

Eyes

A peaked cap or floppy hat and spectacles or sunglasses help protect your eyes from the hooks of artificial flies airborne during a fly-line cast (your cast or the cast of someone else).

I always wear polarizing (anti-glare) sunglasses when fly-fishing, whatever the weather.

For extra safety, wear spectacles or sunglasses with frames that mould in a curve around the side of your eyes.

Keep safely clear of fly-fishers when they are casting.

Clothing

Be wise and always carry a set of heavy duty waterproofs (jacket with hood, and trousers) and pack a spare woollen pullover. A woollen scarf helps prevent icy wind and rain from funnelling down your neck, and in cold weather a pair of *fingerless* woollen or thermal fishing mitts keep your hands warm without interfering with your fly-fishing.

Never be without a peaked cap or floppy hat, and/or a woollen hat in cold weather; much of our valuable body heat is lost through a bare, unhatted head.

A cap or hat also helps protect your head from the hooks of artificial flies airborne during a fly-line cast (your cast or the cast of someone else).

Food

Always pack some warming and nourishing food; sandwiches, flask of hot soup and a couple of chocolate bars.

Apply standards of hygiene for handling food and drink at the waterside similar to the standards you would normally set at home.

Insect repellent
Always carry an adequate supply of insect repellent and apply liberally to escape the unwelcome attention of waterside insects that bite.

First aid notes
Be prepared: carry a basic first aid kit containing assorted waterproof plasters, roll of sterile bandage, safety pins, antiseptic cream and pain killing tablets.

NEVER allow an open cut, scratch or graze to come in contact with *untreated* water, or with any freshly caught fish.

Always wash immediately *(where possible)* any cut, scratch or graze in *treated* tap water; apply antiseptic cream and a waterproof plaster or/and a sterile dressing (bandage).

If the cut, scratch or graze does not heal, or you feel unwell, see your General Practitioner (Doctor), and explain that the accident occurred by the waterside while you were fishing. (Waterborne diseases, e.g. *Leptospirosis*, a form of leptospiral jaundice commonly known as Weil's disease, can be transmitted into the bloodstream through minor cuts and abrasions.)

In the event of serious injury seek *immediate* medical attention.

11

TRADITIONAL
ARTIFICIAL FLIES

The more successful and popular **traditional** dry and wet trout-flies **include:**

Alder: *Dry and wet patterns.* Represents the natural Alderfly *(Sialis lutaria* and *Sialis fuliginosa);* especially effective April–July, fished dry or wet on still or flowing waters.

Alexandra: *Wet pattern.* A general representation of a small fish-fry; especially effective June–October, fished wet on still or flowing waters.

Ant: (Black/Brown/Red): *Dry pattern.* Represents a winged ant (order: *Formicidae*); especially effective July–September, fished dry on still or flowing waters when mating winged-ants swarm.

Bibio: *Wet pattern.* A general representation of a natural fly of the family *Bibionidae* (order: *Diptera*) which includes the Black Gnat *(Bibio johannis),* Hawthorn Fly *(Bibio marci)*, and Heather Fly *(Bibio pomonae).* Especially effective May–September, fished wet on still or flowing waters.

Black-And-Peacock Spider: *Wet pattern.* A general representation of a natural fly/insect (can be used to represent a freshwater snail or beetle); can be effective March–October, fished wet on still or flowing waters.

Black Gnat: *Dry pattern.* Represents the natural fly *(Bibio johannis,* of the order *Diptera);* especially effective May–September, fished dry on still or flowing waters.

Blae and Black: *Wet pattern.* Represents a pupa of the Black Midge *(Chironomus anthracinus,* of the order *Diptera);* especially effective March–September, fished wet on still-waters.

Blue Upright: *Dry pattern.* A general representation of a natural fly/insect. Can be used to represent a Large Dark Olive Dun *(Baetis rhodani),* or Iron Blue Dun *(Baetis niger* and *Baetis muticus)* mayfly, or a Willow Fly *(Leuctra geniculata)* stonefly; can be effective March–October, fished dry on still or flowing waters.

Blue Winged Olive: *Dry pattern.* Represents the natural mayfly *(Ephemerella ignita);* especially effective May–October, fished dry on flowing waters, or still-waters where this mayfly is present.

Brown Silverhorns: *Dry pattern.* Represents the natural sedge-fly *(Athripsodes cinereus);* especially effective June–August, fished dry on still or slow-flowing waters.

Butcher: *Wet pattern.* A general representation of a small fish-fry; especially effective June–October, fished wet (can be successful fished dry!), on still or flowing waters.

Caenis: *Dry pattern.* Represents the natural mayflies called Broadwings *(Caenis & Brachycercus* – six species); especially effective June–August, fished dry on still or flowing waters.

Caperer: *Dry pattern.* Represents the natural sedge-fly *(Halesus radiatus);* especially effective August–October, fished dry on flowing waters.

Caterpillar: *Dry pattern.* A general representation of a caterpillar (larva of butterfly or moth); especially effective May–August, fished dry, near overhanging trees or bushes on still or flowing waters.

Cinnamon Sedge: *Dry pattern.* Represents the natural sedge-fly *(Limnephilus lunatus);* especially effective June–October, fished dry on still or flowing waters. The **Cinnamon and Gold** is often used to represent a pupa of the Cinnamon Sedge, and is especially effective June–October, fished wet on still-waters.

Coachman: *Dry and wet patterns.* A general representation of a natural fly/insect (can be used to represent a sedge-fly pupa when fished wet, or a moth when fished dry). A good all-purpose artificial fly; effective March–October, fished wet or dry on still or flowing waters.

Coch-Y-Bonddu: *Dry and wet patterns.* Represents the natural beetle *(Phyllopertha horticola,* of the order *Coleoptera);* can be used to represent any species of beetle. Effective March–October, fished wet or dry on still or flowing waters.

Corixa: *Wet pattern.* A general representation of an aquatic beetle of the family *Corixae* (about 30 species, commonly called *lesser water boatmen*). Especially effective June–September, fished wet on still-waters (can be fished wet on slow-flowing waters).

Cranefly (also known as **Daddy Longlegs**): *Dry pattern.* Represents the natural cranefly (Genus: *Tipula*, many species); especially effective June–September, fished dry on still or flowing waters.

Daddy Longlegs, see **Cranefly,** above.

Damselfly Nymph: *Wet pattern.* A general representation of the natural nymphs of the Damselflies (order: *Odonata;* sub-order: *zygoptera,* 17 species). Especially effective June–August, fished wet, just below the surface, on still-waters (can be fished wet on flowing waters).

Dunkeld: *Wet pattern.* A general representation of a small fish-fry; especially effective June–October, particularly on large still-waters, fished wet.

Ginger Quill: *Dry pattern.* A general representation of the Pale Watery Dun *(Baetis fuscatus)* and Medium Olive Dun *(Baetis vernus & Baetis tenax)* mayflies. Can be used as a general representation of light-coloured Olive Dun mayflies; effective May–October, fished dry on flowing waters.

Gold Ribbed Hare's Ear: *Dry and wet patterns.* Commonly called "GRHE"; a general representation of the mayflies: Medium Olive Dun *(Baetis vernus & Baetis tenax)*, Large Dark Olive Dun *(Baetis rhodani)*, and Small Dark Olive Dun *(Baetis scambus).* The GRHE can also be fished as a general representation of other mayfly duns, or a mayfly nymph. Effective March–October, fished dry or wet on still or flowing waters.

Grannom: *Dry pattern.* Represents the natural sedge-fly *(Brachycentrus subnubilus);* especially effective April–June, fished dry on flowing waters.

Greenwell's Glory: *Dry and wet patterns.* A general representation of all the Olive Dun mayflies; can be used to represent the Iron Blue Dun *(Baetis niger & Baetis muticus);* can also be fished to represent a mayfly nymph. Effective March–October, fished dry or wet on still or flowing waters.

Grey Duster: *Dry pattern*. A general representation of a natural fly/insect; can be effective March–October, fished dry on still or flowing waters.

Grey Sedge, see **Silver Sedge,** on page 115.

Grouse and Claret: *Wet pattern*. Represents the Sepia Dun *(Leptophlebia marginata)* mayfly; can also be used to represent the Claret Dun *(Leptophlebia vespertina)* mayfly, and the nymphs of both species. Especially effective April–June, fished wet (can be fished dry), on still or flowing waters.

Hawthorn Fly: *Dry pattern*. Represents the natural fly *(Bibio marci);* also known as **St. Mark's Fly**. Especially effective May–September, fished dry on still or flowing waters.

Heather Fly: *Dry pattern*. Represents the natural fly *(Bibio pomonae);* especially effective August–September, fished dry on still or flowing waters where this fly is present.

Hofland's Fancy: *Dry pattern*. A general representation of a natural fly/insect. Can be used as a general representation of a natural sedge-fly (order: *Trichoptera*). Can be effective April–October, fished dry on still or flowing waters.

Iron Blue Dun: *Dry pattern*. Represents the natural mayfly *(Baetis niger & Baetis muticus);* especially effective May–October, fished dry on still or flowing waters.

Kite's Imperial: *Dry pattern*. A general representation of a natural fly; can be used to represent the natural Claret Dun *(Leptophlebia vespertina)*, Large Dark Olive Dun *(Baetis rhodani)*, Medium Olive Dun *(Baetis vernus &*

Baetis tenax), Olive Upright Dun *(Rithrogena semicolorata)*, and Small Dark Olive Dun *(Baetis scambus)* mayflies. Effective March–October, fished dry on flowing waters (can be fished dry on still-waters, as a general representation of a natural fly).

Lake Olive Dun: *Dry pattern.* Represents the natural mayfly *(Cloeon simile);* especially effective April–June, and again August–October, fished dry on still or flowing waters.

Lunn's Particular: *Dry pattern.* Represents the Medium Olive Dun *(Baetis vernus & Baetis tenax)* mayfly spinner, also the Large Dark Olive Dun *(Baetis rhodani)* mayfly spinner. Effective March–October, fished dry on still or flowing waters.

Mallard and Claret: *Wet pattern.* A general representation of a nymph-like creature; can be used to represent a sedge-fly pupa, or a mayfly nymph. Effective March–September, fished wet on still or flowing waters.

March Brown: *Dry and wet patterns.* Represents the natural mayfly *(Rithrogena germanica);* especially effective March–May, fished dry or wet on flowing waters.

Mayfly (also known as **Greendrake**): *Dry pattern.* Represents the natural mayflies *Ephemera danica* and *Ephemera vulgata;* especially effective May–June, fished dry on still or flowing waters.

Midge (Black/Brown/Green/Red; also Golden/Olive/Orange-Silver); *Wet pattern.* A general representation of a non-biting midge (order: *Diptera,* family *chironomidae,* numerous species; commonly called **"Buzzers"** by anglers). The **black midge** can be especially effective March–April, and again July–October; the **brown midge**

June–September; the **green midge** March–October; the
red midge June–September; the **golden midge** June–
August; the **olive midge** May–June, and again August–
September; the **orange-silver midge** (commonly called
"grey boy" by anglers), April–July. Midges are usually
fished wet (can be fished dry) on still-waters. Midges can
be fished wet (or dry), on flowing waters where they are
present. The **Hatching Midge Pupa** can be effective
March–October, fished wet (deep to just below the
surface), on still-waters, or flowing waters where hatches
are occurring.

Moth (White/Brown): *Dry pattern.* A general representation of an insect (moth) of the order *Lepidoptera;*
especially effective June–September, fished dry, at dusk
or after dark, on still or flowing waters.

Olive Dun: *Dry pattern.* Represents the natural Medium
Olive Dun mayflies *(Baetis vernus & Baetis tenax);*
especially effective May–October, fished dry on flowing
waters.

Pale Watery Dun: *Dry pattern.* Represents the natural
mayfly *(Baetis fuscatus);* especially effective May–
October, fished dry on flowing waters.

Palmer (Black/Brown/Grey/Red): *Dry and wet patterns.*
A general representation of a natural fly/insect or beetle;
can be effective March–October, fished dry or wet on still
or flowing waters. Can also be used, fished wet, to
represent a freshwater shrimp, nymph or pupa, or almost
any small aquatic life form.

Peter Ross: *Wet pattern.* A general representation of a
small fish-fry; especially effective June–October, fished
wet on still or flowing waters.

Pheasant Tail: *Dry and wet patterns.* A general representation of a natural fly/insect; can be particularly effective, fished dry, to represent a mayfly spinner of the Blue Winged Olive Dun *(Ephemerella ignita),* Iron Blue Dun *(Baetis niger & Baetis muticus),* Pale Watery Dun *(Baetis fuscatus),* or Medium Olive Dun *(Baetis vernus & Baetis tenax).* Can be effective March–October, fished dry or wet on still or flowing waters. Can also be used, March–May, fished wet, to represent a nymph of the March Brown Dun *(Rithrogena germanica)* mayfly, on flowing waters where this mayfly is present.

Pheasant Tail Nymph: *Wet pattern.* A general representation of a nymph/small fish-fry/aquatic creature; can be effective March–October, fished wet on still or flowing waters.

Red Spinner: *Dry and wet patterns.* A general representation of the female spinners of the Medium Olive Dun *(Baetis vernus & Baetis tenax),* and Small Dark Olive Dun *(Baetis scambus)* mayflies. Especially effective May–October, fished dry or wet on flowing waters. The **Large Red Spinner** represents the female spinner of the Large Dark Olive Dun *(Baetis rhodani)* mayfly; especially effective February–May, fished dry or wet on flowing waters.

Rough Olive: *Dry pattern.* Represents a Large Dark Olive Dun *(Baetis rhodani)* mayfly; especially effective February–May; also September–November, fished dry on flowing waters.

Sand Fly: *Wet pattern.* Represents the natural sedge-fly *(Rhyacophila dorsalis);* especially effective April–September, fished wet on flowing waters.

Sedge (Dark/Medium/Light): *Dry pattern.* A general representation of an adult sedge-fly of the order *Trichoptera;* can be effective April–October, fished dry on still or flowing waters.

Sherry Spinner: *Dry pattern.* Represents the female spinner of the Blue Winged Olive Dun *(Ephemerella ignita)* mayfly; especially effective May–October, fished dry on flowing waters, or still-waters where this mayfly is present.

Shrimp: *Wet pattern.* Represents the natural freshwater shrimp (genus: *Gammarus,* several species); can be effective March–October, fished wet on still or flowing waters.

Silver Sedge (also known as **Grey Sedge**): *Dry pattern.* Represents the natural sedge-fly *(Odontocerum albicorne);* especially effective June–October, fished dry on fast-flowing waters.

Smut: *Wet pattern.* Represents the natural Blackfly (order: *Diptera,* genus: *simulium,* many species); especially effective May–September, fished wet on flowing waters, or large still-waters.

Snail: *Wet pattern.* A general representation of a natural freshwater snail (phylum *Mollusca,* class: *gastropoda,* many species); especially effective July–September (when some species of freshwater snail migrate to the water surface on still-waters), fished wet – just below the surface on still-waters.

St. Mark's Fly, see **Hawthorn Fly,** on page 111.

Tadpole: *Wet pattern.* Represents a natural tadpole (larva of frogs or toads; also newts); especially effective March–

June (when tadpoles mass in shallow water), fished wet on still-waters.

Teal, Blue and Silver (also Teal & Red/Black/Green, etc.): *Wet pattern.* A general representation of a small fish-fry; can be effective June–October, fished wet on still or flowing waters.

Tup's Indispensable: *Dry and wet patterns.* A general representation of the female spinners of the Pale Watery Dun *(Baetis fuscatus)*, Small Spurwing Dun *(Centroptilum luteolum)*, Large Dark Olive Dun *(Baetis rhodani)*, and Medium Olive Dun *(Baetis vernus & Baetis tenax)* mayflies. Can be effective May–October, fished dry or wet on still or flowing waters.

Water Cricket: *Wet pattern.* Represents the natural insect *(Velia caprai,* of the order *Hemiptera);* especially effective March–June, fished wet (can be fished dry), on still-waters.

Welsh Partridge: *Wet pattern.* A general representation of a natural fly/insect; can also be fished wet to represent a nymph-like creature. Can be effective March–October, fished wet on still or flowing waters.

Welshman's Button: *Dry pattern.* Represents the natural sedge-fly *(Seriscostoma personatum);* especially effective June–July, fished dry on still or flowing waters.

Wickham's Fancy: *Dry and wet patterns.* A general representation of a natural fly/insect; can be effective March-October, fished dry or wet on still or flowing waters.

Willow Fly: *Dry pattern.* Represents the natural stonefly *(Leuctra geniculata);* especially effective August–

November, fished dry on stony flowing waters.

Woodcock and Hare's Ear: *Wet pattern.* A general representation of a nymph-like creature; can be effective March–September, fished wet on still or flowing waters.

Yellow May Dun: *Dry pattern.* Represents the natural mayfly *(Heptagenia sulphurea);* especially effective May–August, fished dry on flowing waters, or still-waters where this mayfly is present.

Yellow Sally: *Dry and wet patterns.* Represents the natural stonefly *(Isoperla grammatica),* also the natural stonefly Small Yellow Sally *(Chloroperla torrentium);* especially effective April–August, fished dry or wet on stony flowing waters or stony still-waters.

Zulu (Black/Blue/Gold/Silver): *Wet pattern.* A general representation of a natural fly/insect. The Black Zulu can also be fished to represent an aquatic or terrestrial beetle. Can be effective March–October, fished wet on still or flowing waters.

12

NIGHT FISHING
FOR TROUT

Trout often continue feeding after dusk and into the night.

Trout have good night vision and can see natural flies and insects present at night in, on, or just above the water.

Big trout are especially active at night in their search for food.

We may choose to night-fish locations on rivers, streams, or still-waters, most likely to hold trout in the daytime (see chapter 8); these places could provide excellent sport at night, though to achieve the best possible results from night-fishing consider the merits of other locations after nightfall.

Big trout, emboldened by the protective cloak of darkness, feel sufficiently secure to leave their daytime deep water lies and hideaways, nose the water surface, explore streamy runs of shallow water, and shallow water near the bank or shore.

When night-time is the right time
Night-time is the right time to fly-fish water we may shun in daytime: quiet, nondescript pools, deepish "flat" stretches of water, streamy runs of shallow water, exposed

areas of shallow water, and water near the bank or shore "scared troutless" in daytime by noise, hustle and bustle (near busy car parks, popular picnic and paddling zones, places frequented by holidaymakers and tourists, easily reached fishing spots popular with parades of daytime anglers, etc.).

Areas of water avoided by big trout in daytime, are often investigated by big trout at night.

Artificial flies for night fishing

Any pattern of artificial fly that can catch trout during the day on the water you intend night-fishing, could catch trout on that water at night.

Artificial representations of natural sedge-flies can be especially effective at night, June–September; fished dry on still or flowing waters.

Artificial midge patterns are often effective at night, March–September, fished wet (can be fished dry), on still-waters, or rivers and streams where midges are present.

An artificial representation of a moth can be especially effective at night, June–September, fished dry on still or flowing waters.

Artificial nymphs and pupae can be especially effective at night, (fished wet on still or flowing waters), when a "hatch" of natural flies – notably sedge-flies and midges – occurs and adult flies are emerging on the water surface from their nymphal or pupal skins.

Artificial flies imitating small fish-fry can be especially effective at night, June–October, fished wet on still or flowing waters.

Artificial flies incorporating the colours white or silver can prove particularly successful at night, because white and silver reflect natural night-time light, and attract the attention of feeding trout.

Choose the right night

Night-time fly-fishing may yield poor results on quiet waters bathed in revealing moonlight. Trout seem nervous of feeding and acutely sensitive to the slightest noise or vibration, easily spooked by anglers' moving shadows and uneasy until dawn.

Anticipate good night-time catches of trout when there are moon-obscuring clouds overhead.

The best night-time catches of big trout should be expected when the night is black, particularly when the air is warm and humid ("muggy"), or there is a warm, moist breeze.

Preparation for night-fishing

● Study the water in daytime, note the best places to fly-fish after nightfall.

● Check your fly-fishing tackle is in first-class working order, and wind at least four spare ready-prepared leader lines, artificial flies attached, onto circular cast carriers (see page 70).

● Remember, for your safety, to take a waterproof torch (plus spare bulb and batteries). A battery-operated headlamp can prove a boon when fishing after nightfall; fastened to your forehead by its comfortable headband, the headlamp leaves your hands free and when switched on beams light at whatever you *need* to see (be safe; have your torch handy for extra instant light).

Resolve to make the least possible use of artificial light.

Flashes or beams of light at night scare trout feeding near the bank or shore, and alert other trout to your presence.

● Pack sandwiches, flask of hot soup and a couple of chocolate bars.

● Wrap up in warm clothing *before* travelling to the water

(to trap warm air around your body); pack a spare woollen pullover, set of heavy duty waterproofs (jacket with hood, and trousers), and don't forget your hat!

At the waterside

Arrive near the bank or shore position from which you intend fly-fishing by late dusk, while you can still see – *before* night darkens pitch-black.

Stay well back from the water and quietly assemble your fishing tackle; move forward and begin fly-fishing when your actions are masked by the dark.

BE AWARE: night-feeding trout can glimpse your silhouette moving against the skyline – stand or kneel out of sight.

Big trout could be feeding not far from where you are standing or kneeling. Begin fly-fishing with short casts to water close to the bank or shore.

Should you hear the splashes or "smacking-kiss" sounds of trout feeding at or just below the water surface, judge the direction and distance, make an accurate cast and hook your trout.

Big trout may rove widely and feed at various depths during the course of the night, often beginning at the water surface and in shallow areas of water, then feeding in deeper water as the night progresses and the water temperature drops.

The best night-time catches of big trout are made by fly-fishers who keep silent, reduce movement to an absolute minimum, and persist in fly-fishing the water before them.

For optimum night-time results, aim to fly-fish "blind" throughout the night; use no artificial light (except for *occasional* safety reasons); make no sound. Listen, touch and feel.

When the moon is bright, fly-fish facing the moon, so your shadow does not fall across the water.

Sea trout *(Salmo trutta)*
Night-time is the best time to catch big sea trout on their journey up rivers and streams to breed *(spawn)*.

Sea trout (see chapter 2, page 12) begin to gather in river estuaries round May/June and travel up rivers and streams in shoals, mainly at night, lying low during the day in deep pools and stretches of water overshadowed or screened by trees and shrubs (see also chapter 8, Locating Trout, beginning on page 86).

Sea trout continue to shoal in estuaries and run up rivers and streams until August/September.

Sea trout breed *(spawn)* in the gravel of clear, oxygen-rich flowing water, from October–December, then return to the sea.

The sea trout is especially shy and cautious in the unfamiliar surroundings of freshwater rivers and streams.

To catch big sea trout at night be very quiet, keep low and stay well back from the water's edge.

Traditional sea trout flies
The more successful and popular **traditional** artificial flies for sea trout fishing **include:**

Alexandra (fished wet), Black Palmer (fished dry or wet), Black Zulu (fished wet) Blue Zulu (fished wet), Butcher (fished wet), Cinnamon and Gold (fished wet), Mallard and Claret (fished wet), March Brown (fished dry or wet), Red Palmer (fished dry or wet), Teal and Black (fished wet), Teal, Blue and Silver (fished wet), Teal and Green (fished wet).

1 flat water between rocks   **2** streamy water below falls
3 at the tails of pools

42. River lies of sea trout

Good night

To relax and enjoy a good night's fly-fishing, *expect*
sights and sounds which may defy immediate rational
explanation.

You share the night with creatures hunting food under
cover of darkness: moths, nightjars, owls, bats, rats,
hedgehogs, stoats, moles, badgers, foxes; many life forms

– large and small – moving through the air, on the ground and in the water.

Some nocturnal creatures make *eerie* sounds at night.

I wish you a good night, tight-lines and great sport!

INDEX

125

Other fishing titles by Ian Ball

BEGIN FISHING THE RIGHT WAY

Teaches you how to catch big fish from both freshwater and sea. With descriptions of the plants and creatures you will see while fishing and hints on how to develop your angling skills, this book shows how, on a modest budget, all of us can enjoy this great outdoor sport.

FRESHWATER FISHING PROPERLY EXPLAINED

Of value to beginner and experienced angler, this marvellous book is packed with facts, tips and hints to help you catch more and bigger fish!

SEA FISHING PROPERLY EXPLAINED

Explains all you need to know to begin making expert catches from beach, rock, outcrop, estuary, pier, harbour wall or boat. Understand tides; know the natural foods of different fish species; identify types of seabed favoured and pin-point coastal areas which fish shoals frequent; and learn the right technique to catch large 'specimen' fish.

All uniform with this book

Published in the *Right Way* series by Elliot Right Way Books, Lower Kingswood, Tadworth, Surrey, KT20 6TD, UK.
www.right-way.co.uk